Rail Transport Infrastructure

Steven Boldeman

© Dolans Publishing

National Library of Australia Cataloguing-in-Publication Data
Creator: Boldeman, Steven Author
Title: Rail Transport Infrastructure
ISBN: 978-0-6483093-0-7

Subjects – Railroads – Planning
Transportation – Planning
Transportation - Australia

Dewey Number: XXXX

Dolans Publishing

Table of Contents

Chapter 1 Introduction

Rail systems have seen a tremendous upsurge in interest and construction in the last 10 to 20 years. Across the world many counties are in the process of building many new rail lines. Rail is considered to be something that industrialised nations need, and modern rail systems are seen as a strong indicator of the health and well being of the economy in a country.

Rail systems require large numbers of engineering systems to operate. Rail systems are very asset heavy, and their construction is a very serious engineering project. As a transport system, rail systems are very complex, expensive to build, and require specialised people with specialised skills to properly construct.

This book is no more than a basic introduction to a very large area: rail infrastructure. Rail infrastructure is a broad term that refers to a large and sweeping array of different types of equipment. From software to stations, a modern rail system is comprised of numerous complex systems, all of which need to work together harmoniously to get the rail system to work at peak efficiency.

There are many different types of rail systems, and at the beginning of the book there is a run-through of the different types. Light rail typically has much less by way of infrastructure than heavy rail, although this is changing. Different types of systems and equipment are appropriate for different types of rail systems, and even the most important rail engineering systems, such as signalling and power are not always present in all rail systems. Sugar cane trains, which are a form of freight light rail, have almost no signalling at all, so the engineering is really tailored to the rail need.

Rail tunnels are discussed in depth. Rail tunnels are a very common and yet very expensive part of modern rail system design. The choice as to their configuration play a very important role in the operation of any new rail system.

And of course no book on rail would be complete without a discussion of rail stations. For any passenger rail system, stations are a very central part of the system, and is the place where passengers board and alight. Stations are the focus for a variety of different engineering systems, such as ticketing, passenger information, and fire and safety systems. Stations are discussed in detail.

Chapter 2 Describing a Rail System

The type of rail infrastructure used for any rail system depends on the nature of the rail system. Rail systems come in a variety of different forms, and the rail mode determines the type of infrastructure installed, and how much of it is installed. We cannot sensibly discuss rail transport without first identifying, broadly, the different types of rail systems and how they are described. This is the purpose of this chapter.

There are several commonly used parameters that can be used to almost completely describe a rail system and many of these are described below. Some of them are related to the size of the network, the number of people that use the system, how the system is used by its passengers, and some other useful information.

Number of passengers per day

The size of any rail system is often judged in terms of the number of trips per day. A rail system that moves 10,000 per day is dramatically different to one that moves 1 million per day. Small rail systems can have a lot less infrastructure, compared to a large system that might move 3 million per day.

An alternative name for trips is boardings.

Below is a general guide as to the size of a rail system, and whether it is large or small.

Sizes of rail systems – Number of Passengers		
Trips per day	**Description**	**Comments**
<10,000	Very small	Tourist trains, some tram systems, a small light rail system, an APM in an airport
10,000 to 100,000	Small	High speed rail, most commuter rail systems, small to medium light rail systems
100,000 to 1,000,000	Medium sized	Metros with 2 or 3 lines, large light rail systems, large commuter systems

Sizes of rail systems – Number of Passengers		
Trips per day	**Description**	**Comments**
> 1,000,000	Large	Very large commuter systems, some metros in big cities. No light rail or high speed rail systems move this number of people, nor monorails

Rail as a transport system is capable of moving very large numbers of people. Buses may only move small numbers in comparison, as a reasonable sized bus may move 60 to 100 people, and a commuter train may move a thousand. One of the great advantages or rail systems is the ability to move large numbers of people. A BRT (Bus Rapid Transit) system that has 20 buses per hour, will only move between 1200 to 2000 people per hour for one line in any one direction, and for rail transport this would be considered a very low number. Even the largest BRT systems are small in comparison to a moderately sized rail system.

Route Length

The route length of a rail system is an important metric. Rail systems can be very small, but can also be very effective. A short length system can move very large numbers of people, especially if it is a metro, even it is quite small. Tram and light rail systems often have a very low number of kilometres of route length, whereas a regional rail system can be extremely large.

Route length is normally measured in kilometres, unless it's in North America or the UK. Care needs to be taken in not confusing route length with track length. The route is the rail corridor where the tracks pass through, and there can be more than one track in any rail corridor. Some rail corridors have many tracks, and up to six is quite common, and some places there are more. There are also some places where trains are stored, and this is called stabling. When counting track length, stabling and marshalling yards can add a lot of kilometres, but for route length add very little.

The table below shows how many route kilometres constitute a large or small system. Again, these numbers are just a guide, and are included to give the reader some sense of what a large or small system looks like.

Route kilometres		
Length	**Size**	**Comments**
< 10 kms	Tiny	One metro line, tourist railway, monorail, airport syste m
10 – 30 kms	Very small	One or two metro lines, mostly removed legacy tram systems
30 – 100 kms	Small	Many metro systems, many light rail systems, small commuter rail systems, no high speed rail
100 – 500 kms	Medium	Very large tram or light rail systems, commuter rail systems, smaller high speed rail systems
500 – 5000 kms	Large	Large commuter or high speed rail systems, no metros, light rail, monorails nor trams in this category
> 5000 kms	Extremely large	National rail systems, extensive regional train system

What is large for one system can be small for another. High speed rail systems tend to be large, hundreds of kilometres at least, whereas metros are far smaller.

Number of Stations

The number of stations is a key measure for any rail system. The number can vary enormously, as high speed rail systems may have only a tiny number of stations, for example the high speed rail system in Taiwan only has 8 stations. On the other hand, even small tram or light rail systems can have very large numbers of stations, as every street corner can serve as a station. Tram stops are often only 500 metres apart, and a stop on one side in one direction does not mean that there is a matching tram stop on the other side/direction. A tram system of 10 kilometres may have 20 stations. In a tram system there can be large number of stops.

Even for heavy rail, it is not always clear what constitutes a station for counting purposes. Some stations are only opened at certain times of the year, or for special events. Others, especially ones for horse racing or stadia, are only opened when an event is on. There are also small stations where trains do not ordinarily stop, and sometimes these are called halts. A halt is a stop where passengers need to ask rail staff for the train to stop, otherwise the train does not stop. Passengers who need to board a train from a halt need to signal to the driver to stop, and with some luck, this will happen.

Despite the problems with counting the number of stations in a rail system, most of the time it is a very good measure of the size of a system. In most situations a station can be clearly identified from the surrounding track.

Traffic Type

Many, or maybe most, rail systems move only one type of rail traffic. For example, a tram system moves only trams, and does not move commuter or high speed rail traffic. There are always exceptions to this, and some tram systems used to move freight, and there are still a very small number that still do. The different categories of rail traffic types are:

- Light rail
- Trams
- Freight
- Metros (heavy rail)
- Commuter (heavy rail)
- High speed rail
- Others

It should be noted that a rail system that has both passenger and freight traffic is often described as a "mixed" system.

Power Supply

The source of power for any rail system is a very important parameter for any railway. The choice of power source has a large influence on the type of infrastructure that needs to be built to support rail operations. As a rough guide, electricity is provided for rail services where there are large numbers of train movements per day, or for high speed rail. Freight, regional, overnight and commuter systems often use diesel power.

Many rail systems are powered through electricity. Steam power was once extremely common as a source of power, but has fallen out of favour with its high maintenance and running costs. The trend away from steam and to diesel and electric power took decades, and by the mid 70s most of the steam locomotives had been removed, although in some parts of the world continued to be used for another 10 years or so. Steam locomotives now are only used on tourist lines.

There are other methods of propulsion other than steam, electricity and diesel power. An extremely small number of rail systems still use cables, where the rail vehicle grabs onto the cable and is pulled along. This type of system was once common, and cables run underneath city streets, pulled from a central point called a powerhouse. One of the last remaining cable car systems is in San Francisco, and this system is still manual, so a tram employee (called the gripman) needs to apply a clamp to the cable to get the street car to move.

Most trains are diesel or electric, although there are some tourist trains that are steam powered. Diesel systems use diesel fuel to move trains, and electric systems use power generated far away at a power generator to move. Electric systems can be divided into a number of smaller categories, and these are based on the type of electrical power provided. Each rail system can be identified as using one or more power systems that are typically used in a rail system. Power systems are either AC (alternating current) or DC (direct current). AC is now the standard for new rail systems, although the voltages need to be higher, and in some cases this can present a safety risk, so for light rail and trams DC is still preferred. DC is the older power system that previously was commonly used, but now is being slowly replaced with more cost efficient AC power.

Also with the power system almost always a voltage is specified. Common voltages are:
- 750 volts
- 1500 volts
- 3000 volts
- 25,000 volts

The first three voltages are used for DC, and the last one for AC. There are other more unusual ones, but these are the more commonly used voltages. Specifying the power supply for an electric railway requires stating the voltage, followed by whether the power is AC or DC. So specifying a power system would be something like; 1500 Volts DC, or 25,000 Volts AC. The type of power system in use will further influence the choice of trains that are used on the system, and also may increase or decrease the costs and structure of any tunnels constructed.

Where a system has no electricity supply for traction, and there are many of these, then often the system is described as unwired. Power is needed for stations and lighting, but this may be unconnected to traction power.

Many rail systems deliver power through wires suspended over the train, and power is delivered through to the train through a structure on top of the train called a pantograph. However, another structure is also possible called a "third rail", and for this system power is delivered near the ground. This information is also included in any description of a rail system.

Gauge

The gauge of a railway is the distance between the insides of each rail. Most railways have only one gauge, although there are exceptions, such the Tokyo metro. The most common gauge, the one used in the US and for almost all high speed rail, is standard gauge, which is 1435 mm. This corresponds to 4 foot 8.5 inches. Gauges wider than this are normally described as broad gauge, and narrower than this are described as narrow gauge. Common sizes are 1067 mm (cape gauge), and 1520 mm (Russian gauge).

Gauge Distance

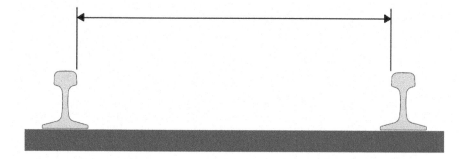

The gauge distance is measured from the inside of each rail to the other. This measure can change a little when the rail is worn, but for reference purposes the gauge is set for one railway (or line as the case may be).

Almost all high speed rail systems use standard gauge. Most modern installations, except where interoperability with older systems is needed, use standard gauge. Standard gauge is the most commonly used gauge, and more than 50 % of the world's railways, in terms of track length, use standard gauge. The use of non-standard gauges will impact upon rollingstock purchases and decisions.

Number of Lines

The number of lines is a useful measure for any railway. A line is a continuous length of track along which passengers can travel without alighting from a train or breaking their journey. In a metro system or a light rail system it mostly very clear how many lines exist, and where lines start and end.

Typically a system with over 6 lines would be considered large, and one with 1 or 2 lines is a small system. Some systems have over a dozen lines.

A commuter system may or may not be described in terms of the number of lines. Commuter lines can converge to a single large station, and there is often shared track where trains from different destinations share the one track. In this situation it can be very difficult to determine how many unique lines there are. In Sydney it is almost impossible to determine how many lines there are as many of the lines meet each other a large distance from the city. Alternatively, in the Go Transit system in Toronto Canada it is very clear how many lines there are because each is mostly separate from each other, and can be easily counted. Again, for a commuter system, more than 6 or 7 lines would be considered a large system.

REFERENCES

1. Zhang, Y & Yan, X & Comtois, C *Some Measures of Increasing Rail Transit Riderships: Case Studies*, Chinese Geographical Science, Volume 10, Number 1, pp 80 – 88, 2000

2. CFL, *Rapport Annuel*, 2011 (In French)

3. Metro de Porto, *Annual Report*, 2009

4. Jernbaneverket, *On Track 2010*

5. State of Florida Department of Transportation, *Central Florida Commuter Rail Transit Design Criteria*, October 2008

6. DB Netze *AG Network Statement 2014,* April 2013

7. Cheng, HY. *High Speed Rail in Taiwan: New experience and issues for future development*, Transport Policy 17 (2010) 51-63, Nov 2009

8. Chun-Hwan, K. *Transportation Revolution: The Korean High-speed Railway*, Japan Railway & Transport Review 40, March 2005

9. Texas Department of Transportation *Austin San Antonio Commuter Rail Study*, 1999

10. Metro de Porto *Annual Report 2011*, http://www.metrodoporto.pt/en/

11. Burge, P. et al Modelling Demand for Long-Distance Travel in Great Britain, www.rand.org, 2011

12. Cataldi, O. & Alexander , R. *Train control for light rail systems on shared tracks*, Railroad Conference 2001

13. Transport for London *Rail and Underground Annual Benchmarking Report* June 2012

14. Prescott, T. *A Practical Scheme for Light Rail Extensions in Inner Sydney*, Transit Australia, vol 63 no 11, 323 – 330 Nov 2008

Chapter 3 Types of Passenger Rail Systems

There are many different types of rail systems, and each has advantages and disadvantages. When one thinks of rail images come to mind maybe of high speed trains or of metros running underneath major cities. The range of different types of rail systems is actually quite large, and the reader might be surprised as to the variety and large differences between them all.

The distinctions between the different types of rail systems is not always clear. Whilst it is easy to distinguish between a freight system, and a commuter one, things are not always so easy. For example, the distinction between a light rail system and a tram system is particularly difficult, as the different types of systems in many cases are quite different, but in others extremely similar. Whilst some tram systems, especially historical ones, appear different to light rail, more modern trams are almost indistinguishable. As such separating out the different types is not an easy task, and an attempt is made here to classify the different rail systems, and it is not possible to consider all the different variations, but nonetheless an attempt must be made.

Rail systems fall under larger headings, and one of those is light rail. This is particularly problematic, as light rail is both a heading and a rail type. This makes things extremely confusing, as the term can refer to either a whole group of different systems, or one particular type of system. The convention that has been adopted to manage this crazy and almost impossible situation in this book is to describe the group of rail systems that fall under the heading of light rail as "light rail systems" and the specific system referred to as light rail as just "light rail".

The choice has been made in this book to separate all the smaller rail systems into the heading of "light rail system". There is no real definition of what this means, especially as a heading, but it is a term commonly used in Australia. It seems clear when looking at the different systems which is a light one, and which heavy, but it is difficult to provide a clear definition. Some of the characteristics of a light rail system include:

- Trains are narrower
- Trains are shorter
- Trains move at slower speeds
- The capacity of any rail lines is lower
- They are physically lighter, and the maximum axle loads can be quite low
- Stations are smaller

- They tend not to have large complex junctions
- They are often much cheaper to construct
- Each individual rail line is quite short, and a maximum line length would be about 30 to 40 kilometres. In contrast high speed rail lines can be hundreds or even thousands of kilometres long.

Alternatively, some light rail systems can be quite expensive to build, especially where the frequency of trains is very high, and the system is driverless. Light rail systems with high capacities can resemble much larger rail systems, and the number of people moved can be reasonably large, ie, one hundred or two hundred thousand per day. The platform heights for light rail systems can also be very low, but in some systems platform height is the same as a heavy rail system.

It is also possible to operate two separate rail systems over the same tracks. Freight trains often share their tracks with regional or commuter trains, and more rarely light rail. Light rail trains can share tracks with heavy rail, so that the infrastructure supports two or potentially more rail systems at the same time. This situation would typically be described as a "mixed system", with at least two different rail systems.

Freight systems can be described as either light rail system or heavy rail classification, and particularly serious rail freight systems, with high axle loads are called "heavy haul".

To the casual observer the type of rollingstock is often the best way to determine which type of rail system is which. Rollingstock has been designed for each different system, and they look different, so this is quite a good way to start. There are however lots of other system parameters that are also relevant, and the top speed is one, and the number of passengers moved is another.

One of the key distinctions between railways is whether they are "at grade" or "grade separated". Grade separation refers to putting different types of transport modes, or even the same ones, at different heights so that traffic on each can pass one another easily, without having to wait for the traffic to clear an intersection before proceeding. The development of light rail, where trains are often at the same grade as road traffic, has changed the perception that grade separation is always necessary for a rail system.

The photo below shows two grade separated metro lines. This design allows one train to pass over another. For high frequency rail services grade separation is the key to ensuring that trains move smoothly. Where one of the lines crosses another at a junction, the junction may be described as a "flying junction" (as it is in this case in Singapore).

Elevated Metros

Another important distinction between rail systems is the ability of some rail vehicles to have articulation. Articulation is the presence of a joint in a vehicle, so that the vehicle can "bend" around corners and curves. Trucks and buses can be articulated, and rail vehicles also. Light rail vehicles may be articulated, to allow them to turn around very sharp curves. Whilst in the past the lack of articulation in trams was an easy way to separate these vehicles from light rail vehicles, some modern trams are articulated as well.

It is sometimes possible to blend two different types of system together. There is no rule that dictates that a rail system must have characteristics from only one type of system, and hybrid systems have been created. Possibly the best known hybrid is the tram-train system that was pioneered in Karlsruhe city in Germany, where trams were re-designed to operate with higher speeds on main line tracks.

Light Rail Systems

Trams

Trams are a very old form of rail transportation. They evolved from the horse drawn carriages that were common in large cities in the mid nineteenth centuries, and were initially steam powered (or pulled by cables). Almost all remaining tram systems in the world are now powered through overhead power lines, where power is supplied from a remote generator to the tram.

Trams are called streetcars in the US and Canada. They are still used in parts of North America, including San Francisco, and Toronto. Trams can be used as simple tourist railways, as they are slow, but a good way of seeing different parts of the centre of a city. Trams may be free in some parts of the centre of large cities, and can be a very pleasing experience to travel on.

Trams were an extremely common system in the Western world until the 1950's, when governments started to remove them. Before their removal they were a central part of the transport for the public for many cities, and some of the tram systems removed were extremely large. The tram system in London was particularly large, and was dismantled with surprising haste in the late 40's and early 50's. Now tram systems are something of a rarity, and very few cities have any kind of remaining tram system. This was particularly the case in the US and Canada, where almost all the old tram systems were removed. Only Toronto and New Orleans operate trams systems that resemble what they were 70 years ago.

In Australia, and the Asia Pacific, the only significant remaining tram system is the one in Melbourne, although there is a much smaller system in Hong Kong that continues to operate for over 100 years. By route kilometres it is the largest remaining tram system in the world, although in the past there were systems that were much larger. The now dismantled system in Sydney was much larger than the one in Melbourne, but has been entirely removed.

Tram systems are rarely double decker (or bi-level) Trams are usually quite narrow, and it is challenging to construct a double decker tram that is both stable and comfortable to use. The trams in Hong Kong are a very rare example of bi-level tram, and offer a quite rough ride.

It is important to distinguish between light rail and tram systems. This distinction is often very difficult to make, but there are significant differences. Light rail is often seen as the logical evolution of tram systems, as light rail is capable of moving more people faster than tram systems. In this book light rail and tram systems are treated as being quite different. Light rail is often contained in separate rights-of way from road traffic, but can have grade separation as well. Light rail vehicles are also longer than trams, wider, and capable of higher speeds and carrying more passengers. Perhaps the most significant difference between trams and light rail vehicles is that trams are have hard chassis with no articulation, and light rail vehicles are longer and can have many articulated sections. Having said that, many trams are now also articulated.

Trams owe their popularity, and demise, to where they operate. They operate down the centre of streets in the middle of major cities, in what in Australia we would call the CBD, but in the US would be described as downtown. They are very slow, but are often filled to capacity. This should be contrasted to the situation with light rail, where trains often run on grade separated tracks, or in the middle or roads where road traffic cannot intrude with their separate right of way.

Loading and unloading times on trams can be very long. As there are only a small number of entrances and exists, overcrowded trams can be very slow in moving off from one stop to the next. Trams are not a very effective mass transit system, for moving large numbers of passengers. They are really too small to move millions of people per day, and are better suited for applications where the number of people moved is modest.

Trams are at the same grade as road traffic, and so collisions between trams and cars are possible, and even common. In one year in Melbourne there were over 1000 collisions between trams and road vehicles. Trams need to be strong enough to withstand a collision with a road vehicle from almost any direction. Whilst the collision between any train and road vehicle is serious, the collision of a heavy rail train and a road vehicle can be catastrophic.

The main differences between light rail and trams are:
- Trams are much shorter than light rail vehicles
- Trams travel down the middle of roads in the centre of cities, something that is often described as being "at-grade", and do not have a separate right of way
- Trams are not connected together
- Trams make a large number of very frequent stops
- Trams are often 2.45 metres wide, whereas light rail is often 2.65 metres wide

Very old trams often look like this one below. This is a W class heritage tram from Melbourne. Note the shape and structure, and that passengers need to step up from the ground to get into the tram. It is also very short, and is only 14 metres in length. It is also rigid, so that there is no articulated section where the tram can bend around corners.

Melbourne W Class tram

Notice that the tram stop has protection for passengers. Passengers wait alongside the fencing, protecting them from road traffic. The gap between the tram and the fence is quite narrow, but this situation is far preferable than having people wait on the side of the road and cross in front of traffic to reach the tram.

The tram shown below is also in Melbourne and was built in the 80's and 90's. It is not single body like the W class, and is articulated to allow it to pass through tight curves. This tram still has high floors, but looks more like a conventional light rail vehicle than older trams. In Melbourne this type of tram is known as a B class tram.

Melbourne B Class Tram

This is a tram stopped on Brunswick St in Melbourne. Notice that there is no dedicated tram stop in the middle of the road, and passengers must cross the road from the kerb to reach the tram. Cars are expected to stop before the end of the tram to allow people to board the tram. This situation, very common in a large legacy tram system like Melbourne, is probably mostly unacceptable in any modern tram system.

It was a common feature of trams that passengers had to step up into the tram and this was a major problem for people with disabilities. There has been a major design effort since the 90's to reduce the height of the floor on trams to make them more accessible for wheelchair bound passengers and others who might struggle to climb the stairs. Trams, and light rail, can be classified as ultra low floor, low floor, or high floor. Whilst the low floor design is popular with passengers, maintenance costs are higher. Ultra-low floor trams and light rail vehicles have been plagued with numerous engineering problems, cracked structures and shells, although things do seem to be getting better for this technology.

High Floor Tram

Passengers boarding this tram will need to climb from the lowest step to the highest. The tram above is considered to be high floor, as for the purposes of determining if this vehicle is low or high floor, it's high floor because this calculation is made from the ground to the floor of the tram where people are sitting, not to the first step.

Low floor trams and light rail vehicles are typically 300 to 350 mm from the ground to the floor of the tram. Ultra low floor trams that distance can be even lower, even as low as 180 mm. High floor trams the distance is often 550 mm or even more. This distance can be reduced by elevating the surface of the road or sidewalk.

It should be noted that many trams and light rail vehicles which are low floor are not consistent height throughout the entire vehicle. The floor above the bogies may be raised, so that passengers moving through the tram will need to walk up and down steps to get from one end to another. This is undesirable from the perspective of passengers with disabilities, but better than having a high floor where disabled passengers can't get on at all. Where the tram is only partly low floor, passengers with limited mobility will need to stay near the doors, as they can't move up and down throughout the steps that are in the vehicle.

The percentage of floor area that is low floor is an important percentage for any tram or light rail vehicle. A typical number seems to be about 70%, although the number can be lower than 50% or up to 100%. This figure is important in purchasing any tram or light rail vehicle.

Given the obvious convenience of low floor trams, why was anything built with a higher floor? Surely it made more sense to design all the trams and light rail vehicles with a low floor? The answer to this is that it was only recently that the technology was available to build a successful a low floor tram. High floor rail vehicles structurally stronger, and trains with higher floors are stronger than those with lower floors. So very long trains, and definitely those over 100 metres in length, will need to have high floors. Even comparatively short trains, such as the DLR or the Bangkok Skytrain, which are only 60 to 80 metres in length have quite high platforms, as it is easier to design trains with higher floors. Rollingstock manufacturers are designing stronger and stronger vehicles, which can combine low floors with longer trains, but there are still limits on the length of these trains.

Note the significant differences between this tram, and the ones above, it has a much lower floor, is articulated in several places, and looks a bit "space age". This particular tram had very few seats, and most of the space inside was for standing passengers. It is also 100% low floor, and there were no steps other than the one into the tram.

Low Floor Tram

The vehicle in the photo above is a good example of rail vehicles that can lie between light rail and trams. Given where the vehicle operates, and its width, and the average speed, its probably best to consider this vehicle operating as a tram, even though there are signs and advertisements throughout Melbourne describing this vehicle as light rail.

The photo below shows tram tracks running down Bridge St in Melbourne. Notice that the street is very wide and that trams and road vehicles have a separated right of way. Trams are free of interference from road traffic, and most of the system in Melbourne is like this. This good design is a key reason why the tram system in Melbourne was able to survive, and it's crucially important for any new tram system to be separated from road traffic as much as possible.

Separate Right of Way for Trams

Most trams are only one level, but there are a small number of systems with double decker trams. Trams in Hong Kong are double deckers. This system is a very old system, and operates wooden double decker trams with two sets of stairs at either end of the tram. There is not much suspension, and it's a very bumpy ride. The cost of a ride is very low, somewhere around 40 US cents (as of 2012), and it's extremely heavily used. These trams operate at amazingly frequent intervals, and there are hundreds of trams in use at any one time.

Double Decker Tram in Hong Kong

The tram system in Hong Kong seems a bit neglected, and there were and still are a lot of ways to improve it. One very significant problem was that tram stops were often not located at traffic lights, but 10 to 30 metres before an intersection. One result of this is that trams stop to let people out, then travel a short distance to the traffic lights, and then stop again. Tram stops should be located at traffic lights, so that when stopped at the lights people can still board the tram, and the tram does not need to accelerate and then stop at the traffic lights.

A modern trend has been to install computer control over traffic lights so that trams get priority. Infrastructure is installed to detect the presence of any tram, and then change the lights to allow the tram to proceed sooner than the normal sequencing of the lights would allow. This situation is particularly common for light rail, where the number of road crossings is much lower than for trams, and the intention is to get the train moving as fast as possible. So doing can substantially increase the average speed of trams, and this is a good way to improve the quality of the system.

An interesting feature of tram systems, and this is especially true for Melbourne, is that often tram stops are marked only with sign, and nothing more. Tram stops are not really stations, and are very low key, and those new to an area with trams may not even notice that the tram stop is there. Stations for other types of rail systems, even light rail, are much larger and more expensive to build.

As a guide for the design of new tram systems, it's best if:
- Trams operate on separate right of ways from road traffic
- Critical intersections are identified and equipment installed to give the tram priority over other road traffic
- Tram stops are located at traffic lights, where there are traffic lights along the tram route
- Passengers are provided with a place to stand next to where the tram will stop
- Trams should be located in central areas of cities or in places where the population density is very high.

(Classic) Light rail

Light rail is seen by many as the next evolutionary step in the development of tram systems. Light rail vehicles are usually larger and longer than trams, and several vehicles can be combined into one longer train, something that is unusual for trams. Whilst there does not seem to be any formal definition anywhere that supports this rule, it seems that light rail vehicles are normally 2.65 metres in width, which is larger than the 2.4 metres common for trams.

Light rail vehicles are designed to travel along city streets. They can climb steep grades, and turn through very tight curves, much like trams. They are a very versatile train type, and can go almost anywhere. Light rail vehicles can climb grades of 10%, and almost unthinkable grade, and far more than any other rail system other than a ratchet and pinion rail line. Light rail vehicles can also negotiate around very tight curves, and curve radii of as low as 20 or 30 metres is possible. Heavy rail is often limited in the size of the curve, and a typical lower value for the tighest curve is 200 metres.

The picture below shows the light rail vehicle moving through central Sydney. Notice that it is a larger and wider vehicle than the trams pictured above. Whilst trams are often only 25 to 40 metres in length, light rail vehicles can be much longer than that, up to 60 metres, and can be coupled together to form even longer trains. This particular light rail vehicle is not designed to be coupled with other light rail vehicles.

Light Rail in Sydney

Once again we note that light rail vehicles can operate on city streets, and building a rail line with a shared right of way with road traffic can be a very effective way to save money on construction costs. As always it is better if the rail line is separated from road traffic as this allows average speeds to be higher, as there is no need for light rail trains to stop for road traffic, although achieving this is sometimes very expensive and not economic.

It is important to distinguish between classic light rail, and an intermediate capacity metro. The DLR (Docklands Light Rail) is often classified as light rail, and it is a light rail system, but it is much more like an intermediate capacity metro, and has many of the features of one. It is not considered to be classic light rail within this book. The DLR is fully automated and there are no drivers, and it does not operate down city streets, but is fully grade separated. The DLR is a very good system, re-classifying it as an intermediate capacity metro is no insult. This type of system will be discussed further below, under the correct heading.

Light rail vehicles traditionally have drivers, important because light rail vehicles need to avoid street traffic, and collisions. At the time of writing it is not possible to design a light rail system that is able to avoid street traffic and pedestrians in all situations, so drivers are needed. Light rail vehicles are designed to be able to withstand an impact from a road vehicle, and are toughened up to resist collisions and not allow any injury to the passengers inside. This toughening can add a lot of weight to the vehicle.

Light Rail in Hong Kong

Light rail has become very popular in the US, and in Germany, although it exists in many different countries. The pictures above and below show a light rail system in Hong Kong. Note that the system used there has high platforms and vehicles are not joined (amalgamated) together to make longer trains.

One of the main attractions of light rail systems is the relatively low construction cost. Costs are lower because the light rail trains travel along city streets, and expensive tunnelling can be avoided. Light rail is also a solution where the number of passengers is not that high, and there is a need or desire to install a rail system. Heavy rail systems are excessive in many situations, and a light rail system can be a more appropriate solution. Aside from the lower construction cost, light rail is seen as a sexy and attractive looking system, and this type of rail system has proved very popular with passengers throughout the world.

An added advantage of the light rail system is its simplicity. Unlike heavy rail, which is technically very complicated, light rail is a lot simpler and easier to install and manage. Lower speeds, and the lower loads associated with smaller trains, means that the system is relatively simple to install, and the complexity associated with speed calculations and vertical curves for example is avoided.

Automated People Mover

Automated people movers (APMs) are automatic trains that are driverless, and operate on separate right of way with grade separation. They are often very small and often installed in airports, theme parks, and other large facilities. These vehicles fall within the family of light rail systems, and are common in airports in Asia. Also sometimes included in this category are larger automatic trains such as the Docklands Light Rail (DLR), which is driverless, and technically speaking an automated people mover. Larger APMs are very similar to light metros, or intermediate capacity systems, and are also discussed under that category.

The picture below shows an APM in Singapore. The vehicle is very short, and it runs on rubber tyres. It is also driverless, and moves around the small network by itself picking up and dropping off passengers. This particular system is a contained within an airport. The capacity of this system is not large, and the distances travelled are short.

An APM Vehicle in Singapore Airport (Changi)

Airports often have trains that move travellers from one terminal to another. A particular large airport may need such a system, as the distances between terminals are so large that transport is needed. These rail systems can be quite significant, and the system in Hong Kong Airport contains two short lines. The APM in Changi airport has several lines, all of them quite short. APM systems in airports are provided as a convenience for passengers, and add to the value of the airport. APMs also exist in theme parks, particular large ones such as the different Disneyland parks.

Intermediate Capacity Metros

Intermediate capacity metros are a system that is designed much like a metro system, with few seats, low headways, and many doors to allow fast and easy boarding and alighting, but much lower capacity and smaller trains. Some intermediate capacity metros are also Automated People Movers, some are not. As a group these rail lines are sometimes described as a "light metro".

What distinguishes an intermediate capacity system from a full metro is:
- Trains are less than 60-70 metres in length
- The trains narrower than full metros
- Stations are much shorter in length, therefore cheaper to build
- In some cases built with rubber tyres rather than metal wheels, although there are some full sized metros with this technology too

Intermediate capacity metros seem to be increasing in popularity, and their numbers are slowly increasing. There are a few rail systems of this type of system in Asia, and the Bangkok Skytrain is probably the best example. The picture below shows a train in the Bangkok Skytrain.

Bangkok Skytrain

There is much to recommend these systems. They are often extremely cheap to build, and well below the cost of a metro system. The Bangkok Skytrain was constructed at a cost of only $20 million per route kilometre, and amazingly low price, and this cost was achieved 2009 to 2011, relatively recently. Trains in an intermediate capacity metro are also very short, 50 to 60 metres is common, and costs are kept down so purchasing rollingstock is very cheap. Stations in an intermediate capacity metro are also short, and an 80 metre station would be considered large. As such it is easy to place stations in convenient places, as they are so short. Stations are also cheap to build.

Intermediate capacity metros would normally be classified as light rail systems. Recall with light rail systems, the lower capacity of this type of system means that the total capacity in people per hour is lower than a metro. A medium capacity system will usually have less than half the capacity of a metro, maybe even a third, and so there is a significant risk of severe overcrowding. Intermediate capacity metros often operate full, even late at night and on weekends. This type of system is attractive to use because of its cost and versatility, but is frequently overcrowded, a trade-off that is sometimes worth making.

Intermediate capacity metros are commonly installed on concrete viaducts, which makes them cheaper than tunnelled full size metros or at least in South East Asia that seems to be the case. It seems common to install this type of system in elevated viaducts, and this also reduces the cost compared to tunnelling. Intermediate capacity systems can operate at very low headways, similar to metros.

Freight Systems (Light Rail)

Freight trains are rarely small enough to be considered light rail, but in a small number of cases they do exist. Sugarcane railways are where sugarcane is transported from the farm to a sugar mill, and these freight systems are often, but not always, operated on 2 foot gauge (61 cm). This is the smallest gauge in operation in a rail system in any significant way at the time of writing of this book. The locomotives and freight wagons are much smaller than traditional freight trains, and their signalling systems are very simple indeed.

The photo below shows some wagons transporting sugar cane in Northern Queensland. Notice that the wagons are very small, and maybe only 3 to 4 metres in length. The ones in the photo below are fully loaded and on their way to the mill.

Sugar Cane Wagons

Small rail freight trains in some mines were also common, but the author is not aware of any that have continued in operation, although they were once common in Australia.

Heavy Rail

Heavy rail systems have much longer trains, move more people faster, and longer distances. It would be very surprising for a light rail system to move passengers one hundred kilometres from one large city to another. Heavy rail systems are more expensive to build, and ordinarily require a larger space (structure and loading gauge).

Metros

Metros are the mainstay of many transport systems. There are hundreds of metro systems installed around the world, and they have been installed in places such as Algiers and San Juan in Puerto Rico. Many more systems are currently being built.

The metro has become the standard for transport around large cities. The metro system forms the backbone of any transport system in many large cities, and bus lines and other forms of public transportation integrate into the rail system. The key to the success of the metro is its ability to move large numbers of people quickly and efficiently from one place to another, as well as its engineering simplicity, and relatively low cost of operation.

Metros almost always have very few seats. People need to stand most of the trip, and consequently many people can be packed into a metro. More people stand than sit, as seating takes up a lot of space. The number of people that can be moved by a large metro is extremely large, over 70 thousand pph (people per hour) in one direction, and this can be done at relatively low cost. The ability of a metro system to move such large numbers of people quickly is one of the key reasons why this system has become so successful. The cost of operating a metro system can also be low when compared to the number of people moved, and in very busy cities it may be possible to operate a passenger service at a profit, without any kind of government subsidy.

Metro trains also have a large number of doors. Metro rail carriages are never double decker (bi-level) and so can have large numbers of doors. Dwell time is an important parameter for many rail systems, and it is defined as the time a train spends at any one station waiting for passengers to alight and board. The minimisation of dwell time is critical to getting trains through a rail system quickly, and on many different types of system, especially commuter systems, the dwell time can be very long. Metros have very low dwell times because doors are numerous and people can move into the train quickly as most people stand. The low dwell time of metros is another contributor to their success.

Inside a Metro

The picture above shows a metro train in Hong Kong. As with many metro trains, there are seats along the side of the train, and none in the middle. This allows a very high concentration of people in the train.

Metro trains mostly move along a single line, starting at one end, finishing at another, and then returning along the same path. More unusually, the metro line may bifurcate, and split into two, with maybe half the trains going to one terminus, and the other half to the other. This is different from a commuter system, or a light rail system, which often has a main station where many of the services converge, and passengers can make their way from one service to another quickly and easily. Metro lines do not converge to a central terminus, and so passengers that need to use more than one line must change trains at a large interchange station. These interchange stations usually have the metro lines passing over and under one another, so that passengers need to use stairs or escalators to move up and down to get to the right platform. This is one of the main disadvantages of metro systems, but can be managed quite effectively with good station design.

Metros have high service reliabilities. Metro trains are almost always on time, mostly due to the simplicity of the system, and that metros operate grade separated from other road and rail traffic. As metros run backwards and forwards all day, from point A to B and then back again, there is very little track infrastructure needed and so there are very few engineering failures. A metro can be compared extremely favourably with commuter rail systems which are often plagued with problems and are frequently late. An on-time-running (OTR) figure of over 99% is the minimum for a properly maintained and operated metro.

Metro trains are not physically very high. Commonly 3.5 metres in height from the bottom of the wheels to the top of the roof would be considered normal for a metro train. This allows tunnelling costs to be significantly reduced, as the size of the tunnel that needs to be excavated is smaller than for commuter trains, especially double decker commuter trains.

Metros can move immense numbers of people. Most rail systems can only move 10 to 15 thousand people per hour (pph) in one direction, but metros can move 60 to 80 thousand in an hour. Some metro lines in Asia and other countries can move over 1 million passengers per day, a truly enormous figure.

Metro systems can have a powerful effect on transport within a city. A good quality metro can clear the roads and allow cars to move through cities very effectively. Even a small number of metro lines can have this effect, and 3 or 4 metro lines is usually enough for cities with even 5 to 6 million people. Hong Kong, which has 4 metro lines (as of 2017) and some other lines that are basically commuter lines, is well served. The same can be said for Taipei, where the city has effectively 3 metro lines and one medium capacity line (although they claim there are many more lines than that, essentially there are three main ones). The utility of metro lines is often very high, and even a small number can transform transport within a city.

Metros are not as suited for long distance travel. As most passengers stand, a journey that takes hours would require passengers to stand for hours, and many people can't or won't do this. High speed and regional trains are never metro trains. So the question arises as to how far passengers will be able to stand when travelling on a metro line, and whilst no one seems to have written or researched this topic, perhaps the answer should be about 1 hour.

Metro lines seem to be getting longer and longer. Traditionally metro lines where quite short in length, and lengths of 10 to 15 kilometres were common. For example, the longest line in the Paris metro is only 24 kilometres long. The author used to believe that one of the lines in Shenzhen was far too long , at 41 kilometres in length, and then another line was constructed in New Delhi that was 49 kilometres long, and another line is under construction in Malaysia that is 51 kilometres long. There is even a line being extended in Shanghai, which was completed in 2010, which is over 61 kilometres long.

The reader should remember at this point that metros typically average 35 kms/hr as an average travel speed, which can be higher or lower depending on the spacing of stations. A metro line that is 60 kilometres in length may require someone to stand for 2 hours to get from one end of the other, and even more if they need to change trains and use another rail line. Older people and those with disabilities will have difficulty in completing this type of journey, as standing for hours may be difficult or even impossible.

The picture below is of a metro station in Taipei. This type of open layout for a metro station is a little unusual. Note the platform screen doors.

A Busy Metro Station in Taiwan

Metro systems may or may not have drivers. Older systems will have drivers, but a more modern approach has been to build systems that are entirely automatic and require no drivers. As metro trains are usually captive along one line, and underground, it is relatively easy to program a computer to drive the train. Often rail staff are on board the train, and may control some aspects of the train operation such as opening and closing doors and making announcements. In this case rail staff are described as "operators" rather than drivers.

The design of stations in a metro system is very important. The large number of people present in the system, and on each train, means that it is very important to get people on and off trains quickly. The key to designing a good metro station is to allow people to move freely in both direction, and this often involves separating passengers walking through the station in different directions. The correct design of stations is very important for metro systems, as most stations are underground, and so there is a rick of fire. Also the large number of people using the system means that dwell times can be very large is the station is not designed with care.

Metros can operate at very short headways, 2 ½ minutes is common. Another common headway between successive trains is 5 minutes. This extremely high frequency of trains contributes much to the popularity and convenience of metro systems.

Commuter/Suburban rail

Commuter rail is a rail system where passengers are moved from an outlying area into the centre of a city, and then back out again. Commuter rail is often considered a rail system for working people, as most trips occur on weekdays. Commuter trips are often from suburban stations far from the centre of the city, to the business centre, and then back out again at the end of the working business day.

Commuter trips are often 1 hour or more in length. Commuter trains have lots of seats, and are not metros, so most people are not expected to stand. It is often the case that people stand on a commuter train, but often this is only for the last few stops before the train reaches the centre of the city.

Commuter trains differ significantly from metros. Commuter trains often travel at higher speeds than metros, a common maximum speed for a metro is 90 kms/hr, whereas commuter trains often reach speeds of 130 kms/hr or even faster. Commuter trains are larger, heavier, and longer and often longer than metro trains. The additional speed requires a heavier and more powerful train. Commuter trains also have extensive seating.

The train below is a commuter train in Brisbane (in Australia). This one is on an elevated concrete viaduct, and at Brisbane airport.

Commuter Train on a Viaduct in Brisbane

Commuter trains can be either single or double deck. Double deck trains are common for commuter trains, especially in Europe, and also the US and Canada. Double deck trains can be an effective way of increasing the capacity of a rail line, as more passengers can be seated for one carriage. Double deck trains are used extensively in the Sydney rail system as well.

The photo below is of a double decker train in Paris.

Parisian Double Decker Train

Commuter trains may operate on a large number of different stopping patterns. The stations that a service stops at is called the stopping pattern, and there are many different possible combinations of stopping patterns even on quite simple lines. A metro system, and light rail, trains almost always stop at every station. With any commuter line there are sometimes stations where very few people board and alight from, and so not every train needs to stop there. Commuter trains, because of the large distances they travel, will need to travel as quickly as possible, and not stopping at smaller stations can reduce the travel time. This is common with commuter systems.

The need for up to date information on a commuter line is very important. Again, as commuter services may not stop at every station, passenger information systems need to display where the train will stop, and when it will arrive at the station. As commuter systems can be very complex, and therefore difficult to understand for passenger, and trains can move in many different directions, providing prompt and accurate passenger information is very important in a commuter system, as it is in any rail system.

The photo below shows the inside of a commuter train in Brisbane. This configuration is 2 x 2, and most of the space inside the train is taken up by seating.

Inside a Single Deck Commuter Train

Commuter systems often have a large central station where all the commuter rail services converge. Easily the most famous of these is Grand Central Station in New York, which has the largest number of platforms of any station in the world (but not the largest number of passengers). Metro systems do not converge to a single station, and this is a good way of distinguishing the difference between the two different types of rail system.

Commuter rail systems often have much more rail infrastructure than metros and light rail. At the commuter main station there are many tracks that carry trains to the station, and many points to move trains to the right platforms. The infrastructure at a main station can often be very expensive to install and costly to maintain.

In a small number of commuter systems, trains carriages are split between 1st and 2nd class. Different fares are charged for each, and more comfortable seating is provided in 1st class. Hong Kong has such a commuter rail line (it's not really a commuter line, as it goes to the border with mainland China, but close enough) with two classes. Passengers in 2nd class get metro style seating, which is very limited and not comfortable at all, and in 1st there are quite "standard" fabric seating in a 2 x 2 arrangement. The fare for 1st class is double that for 2nd class.

Again, comparing commuter systems to metros, most commuter rail systems operate above ground. In the centre of the city, there are sometimes some commuter stations below ground, but most stations away from the centre of town are above ground. Commuter systems are longer and larger compared to metros, and can be over 500 routes kilometres in length. The commuter system in Sydney is over 800 route kilometres in length.

Commuter systems almost always have drivers. The long distances commuter trains travel makes automation difficult, and drivers are almost always used. There may be other staff on the train as well, for example a guard who opens and closes doors, or a ticket conductor that goes through the train and sells tickets of checks passengers have paid for tickets. Commuter trains are more difficult to drive than metros, within the rail corridor many things can happen that require intervention by a driver. There can be landslips, or animals on the track, or trespassers. Trees may fall over onto the track when winds are high.

Commuter systems may share rail tracks with freight, commuter trains operate at low frequencies and over long distances, and so it is often not economical to separate commuter lines from freight ones. Commuter lines that share tracks with freight trains as well typically have a lower capacity.

Commuter trains mostly do not have toilets, unlike regional services. Commuter trips are typically about 1 to 1.5 hours and this is considered short enough that toilets do not need to be provided.

Commuter systems can have a very low service frequency, and one train every 20 or 30 minutes or is quite common. In some systems one train every hour is considered acceptable. Passenger information becomes very important in this environment, as passengers need to plan to meet the train they need.

Regional rail

Regional rail services are those that move from a large city or town to remote or rural towns or villages. They can be, but often are not, commuter services, and regional services can have travel time of up to 3 or 4 hours. Regional services can be very infrequent, from one every half an hour to one per day. Regional services always have a driver, and maybe other staff on the train. Some regional services may have toilets, or even a buffet car where light refreshments can be ordered.

In Australia regional services often pass through areas of national park and wilderness, where there are large numbers of animals and very few people. Collisions with animals are frequent. There is often no mobile phone reception for large parts of the trip for regional services.

Sydney Regional Train

The photo above is a regional train. Note the clear differences with the other doubler decker trains displayed earlier, the much smaller doors, and the greater overall length of the carriage. Loading and unloading of passengers can be very slow for a regional train, but that doesn't necessarily matter because regional services move only moderate numbers of passengers, and the trip length is commonly 3 to 4 hours. It is preferable to design small doors because this increases the structural strength of the train. Carriages in a train designed for regional services can be very long because this reduces the overall cost of procuring the train.

Regional services can be powered by either electric power, or propelled by diesel motors. Many regional services are diesel powered, as there is relatively little rail traffic on many regional lines, and the cost of installing overhead power cannot be justified. Where trains are powered by diesel, then a refuelling depot is needed to top up trains when they run low on fuel.

The photo below was taken at Southern Cross station in Melbourne. This regional train was destined for Albury. Non-driven carriages, drawn behind a locomotive, are referred to as coaches. This configuration is often used for regional services as it is cheaper then electric multiple units (EMUs), or diesel multiple units (DMUs)

Melbourne Diesel Hauled Regional Train

Regional services may operate with very few passengers, and as such don't generate a lot of revenue. Many regional services are provided as a community service, and so are not profitable, and need government subsidies to continue to operate. The regional services that the author has seen in Asia, such as in Thailand, Taiwan China and Malaysia, and in Australia are often dirty and not really very pleasant at all, but provide a basic service to those living in remote places with small numbers of people.

High Speed rail

High speed rail (HSR) is a flashy, sleek and sexy system that is the glamorous side of rail transport. High speed rail is often defined as being any rail system where the train reaches 200 kms/hr, or 125 miles per hour.

High speed rail can be divided into two broad categories; trains/systems where trains travel at less than 250 kms/hr but over 200 kms/hr, and those that travel above that. Below 250 kms/hr, HSR trains are sometimes diesel powered, and do not have the extreme aerodynamic streamlining that gives high speed trains their futuristic look. The more sophisticated high speed rail systems all have top speeds in excess of 250 kms/hr, alternatively HSR rail vehicles that use existing lines have top speeds mostly below 250 kms/hr. Some high speed trains are designed to tilt, although most are not. At high speeds tilting as a strategy is not effective for high speed trains.

Below is a high speed train in Taiwan. High speed trains in Taiwan are based upon a Japanese design (as of 2012) and based on the 700 series Shinkansen.

Taiwan High Speed Train

High speed rail is offer a very high level of service. Its speed and convenience often contribute to this perception. The installation of high speed rail often refreshes and renews the rail system in a country or region. High speed rail sometimes codeshares with airlines, so that passengers can buy a ticket that combined flights and rail trips.

While most high speed trains are single deck, there are a small number of double deck high speed trains. The Japanese have the E4 Shinkansen, and the French have the TGV duplex, but other than those specific trains, all other high speed trains are single deck. Double deck trains have higher capacity, which can be important where route capacity is limited.

High speed trains are almost always powered through overhead power, at 25 kV AC. DC power cannot propel trains at high speeds, as high voltages are needed, and diesel trains can only reach about 250 kms/hr, with difficulty. The higher voltages are needed to drive trains to higher speeds.

High speed trains can be very comfortable. The rail infrastructure that supports the train, such as the track, sleepers and ballast, needs to be very strong and in very good condition so that trains can operate smoothly. This results in a very smooth ride quality that provides very little sensation of movement to passengers. Walking around the train is easy, because the ride is so smooth, and some high speed trains have buffet or dining cars where passengers can get meals.

It is a great achievement for a country to install a high speed rail system. Despite the volume of discussion in Australia and other countries concerning high speed rail, very few systems have been installed. There is only one small high speed line in the US, and it operates at around the 200 kms/hr mark, and so does not have the glamour of the French or Japanese systems. Even in the UK there is only one dedicated high speed rail line, which links the Chunnel to London.

Countries where there are significant high speed rail systems, in 2012, include:
- France
- Germany
- Spain
- China
- Japan
- South Korea
- Taiwan

Other countries have smaller parts of a high speed rail system, one such country is Sweden, where a lot of research has been conducted into high speed rail, despite the small size of their high speed system. The line between Moscow and St Petersburg also has some high speed trains, but the line is shared with freight, and this reduces the average speed and the route capacity.

High speed rail systems face many technical challenges. High speed trains are moving too quickly to move through curves quickly, and can only move through very high radius curves. This often means that high speed rail systems cannot move around mountains and other obstacles, so the rail line often passes through mountains and over other natural obstructions. The alignment of a high speed rail line is very inflexible, and the line can only be designed around any kind of natural barrier with great difficulty.

Tunnels present all sorts of problems for high speed trains. Tunnel design requires the consideration of air movement caused by the train as it moves through the tunnel. The pressure of the air in front of the train is higher than behind the train, and the faster the train moves the worse this problem gets. The pressure drop can cause discomfort to passengers, as the pressure inside the train will equalise with the pressure alongside the train. Rapid changes in air pressures will cause passengers to experience pain in their ears. What is commonly done is to seal the train as much as possible, but even so the seals are not perfect, so the pressure will drop in the train as it passes through a tunnel. Sealing the train can reduce the impact of pressure changes to passengers, but in particularly long tunnels the pressure drop will be significant, even in a well designed train.

High speed trains moving through tunnels can cause an effect often described as similar to sonic boom, and the boom is generated at the exit of the rail tunnel. A high speed train entering the tunnel will generate a pressure wave, which creates the sonic boom. A number of design features can be installed into tunnels to attempt to mitigate this problem, but the most effective strategy is to reduce the speed or the increase the cross-sectional area of the tunnel through which the train is moving. In many cases neither of the strategies will be available.

High speed trains in Taiwan and Japan have very interesting ticketing systems. One feature of these systems is that passengers can buy either first or second class tickets, and first class is more comfortable than second class. But the major difference with "normal" ticketing is the difference between a reserved seat and a non-reserved seat. Reserved seats are those where a seat number is allocated, and these are more expensive that non-reserved. The risk with a non-reserved ticket is that a seat is not available, and it is possible that a passenger may have to stand for part or all of their trip.

High speed rail systems may have services with different stopping patterns. All stops trains alternate with express services, and passengers will want to take the service that takes the minimum time to get to their destination. Prices can be different between HSR services with different stopping patterns, those trains with more stops are cheaper.

Given the appeal and popularity of high speed rail, it is surprising that more of these systems have not been installed. High speed rail competes effectively where the total travel time between one major city and another is 3 hours or less. High speed rail is particularly effective where the travel time is 2 hours or less. When this is so, high speed rail can be so dominant that air services between the two cities is discontinued, for example, Paris and Brussels. Where the travel time is less than 3 hours but more than 2 between cities, then air services will continue but will have a small percentage of the overall market.

Where the travel time is over 4 hours, high speed rail is no longer competitive with air travel. The trip time is simply too long. Many (or most, depending on the type of engine) planes travel at approx 850 kms/hr, less for turboprop planes, and at that speed a trip of 1000 kms is slightly over an hour. For a high speed train, for a top speed of 300 kms/hr, longer journey distances can. High speed rail will only have a small percentage of the market for trips of this length.

Long Distance Rail

One type of rail system that is often forgotten is the long distance rail system. This book uses this title for this type of rail system, but in truth there is no universally accepted definition for this type of system. This category applies for trains that travel over 5 or 6 hours to get to their destination, or even longer. In Australia the train trip from Sydney to Perth takes 3.5 days.

Long distance services are often overnight, and passengers sleep on them. More expensive tickets offer passengers a sleeper berth, and they may sleep in comfort on the train. In some cases a full bed is provided. The experience in Australia has been that sleeper berths are easily the most popular option for long distance rail, despite their additional cost, and are always booked out before other ticket classes.

Below is a photo of a travel compartment in a sleeper carriage in the long distance train that travels from Kuala Lumpur to Singapore. Long distance travel is still somewhat common in Malaysia, and sleepers are available on many night time trains. In a private room there are two bunk beds, as well as a toilet and shower.

Sleeper Compartment in Malaysia

Long distance services are common in Australia, as the distances are so large. There are a number of train services where travel takes well over a day, and these trips can get very boring. The author's experience of this trips is that many of them are rather dull.

Where a rail line has not been upgraded to HSR, or even to a reasonable speed, then overnight distance trains are common. For passengers sleeping on the train makes the trip appear to pass faster, even though it is still a long trip. To justify having sleeper berths on trains, the travel time needs to be at least 7 hours, but preferably 9. Otherwise passengers will have an interrupted sleep, and arrive at their destination at an early time in the morning. For example, a train that leaves at 9pm, and takes 6 hours to reach its destination, will arrive at 3am in the morning. Unless passengers are allowed to stay and sleep in their beds then many will be unwilling to wake at this time in the morning.

Where the train trip is especially long, and the rail operator has made an attempt to upgrade the service, then sometimes the long distance trip is referred to as a rail cruise. A rail cruise can be extremely expensive, thousands of US dollars, and can be over 10 thousand US dollars for 2 people.

A rail cruise is often slower than a normal long distance service, and may stop for a time in different cities, and provide tours to places of interest in the city. This kind of service is rare in Australia, but the small number of services provided are profitable, and it's a rare example of a rail company operator generating a healthy profit. In Australia a company called Great Southern Railways provides rail cruises that are very long, in some cases 21 days, and their trains travel all over Australia. These cruises are very expensive, and are more similar to ocean cruises than rail a service.

Long distance overnight trains that offer sleeper berths seem to be disappearing, especially from Europe. Only a very small number of people can be moved in a sleeper carriage, in one sleeper carriage in Malaysia, the capacity of the carriage was 12 people, a very small number. Sleeper carriages are rarely economical to operate, and the cost to passengers to have a separate cabin with beds can be very high. The role and significance of overnight travel seems to be shrinking.

Other Rail Systems

Monorails

Monorails are normally classified as a type of rail system even though monorails systems are significantly different to almost all other rail systems. Monorails were a popular transport system in the 80's but have since fallen out of favour. There are many monorail systems installed in the world, and possibly the most significant is the commuter monorail system in Tokyo, which connects Haneda airport with the rest of Tokyo city. This monorail moves more people than any other monorail in the world per day. Kuala Lumpur also has a monorail line, which is very heavily used.

Maglev systems are a type of monorail, but are discussed separately below. Maglevs differ from monorails in the way the rail vehicle is propelled.

Mumbai in India has constructed a new monorail line, although their enthusiasm for monorails seems to have waned.. Whilst monorail systems are still being built, they are mostly installed in airports, theme parks and other entertainment related venues, such as casinos and hotels. Serious commuter monorails are rare, and there may be only 20 in the entire world. Overall the experience with monorails has not been a happy one, and several monorails have been installed, only to be removed later. Bankruptcies and failed companies are common with monorail systems.

Monorails can perform very similarly to any other rail system. Rubber tyred monorails can climb grades of up to 6% and top speeds of 80 to 90 kms/hr seem common. Monorails are most comparable to intermediate capacity metros, as they travel at about the same speeds, and carry similar number of people. They also cost about the same amount of money per route kilometre. The system under construction in Mumbai has an estimated cost of only US $22 million per kilometre (2012 dollars), which is a good price, but similar to what was paid for the Skytrain in Bangkok.

The picture below is of the Kuala Lumpur monorail. The vehicle length is rather low, but it is a very effective rail system and moves large numbers of people, despite its short length.

A Monorail in Kuala Lumpur

One criticism of monorails is that the monorail itself, what the monorail vehicle runs on, is unsightly. Another way of saying the same thing is to describe the monorail as visually intrusive. This is true, although not as visually intrusive as an intermediate capacity metro, built on an elevated system.

Monorails are for all practical purposes intermediate capacity systems. The capacity of a single monorail is unlikely to be more than 500 people, which is about the limit for light rail and intermediate capacity metros. A small number of monorails are able to carry thousands of people in one train, as a full metro can.

The high frequency of failure of monorails as a system is somewhat baffling. As a transport system they are safe, and cheap to build, and operate at reasonable speeds. It is surprisingly that monorails have been so unsuccessful in so many cases. Perhaps some reasons for the many failures of monorails are:

- Monorails compete with light rail and intermediate capacity metros, such as the DLR, or the Bangkok Skytrain, and do not quite perform as well
- Monorails cannot be expanded to have the same capacity as full metros
- Monorails cannot travel large distances, as most passengers stand when travelling on a monorail
- The ride quality in a monorail is not quite as good as light rail or metros
- Many monorail systems suffered from excessive political interference, especially during the planning stage
- Many monorails had a very low design capacity, and so were unlikely to ever generate a profit
- Transport orientated development is more difficult with elevated monorail stations, as they are smaller, reducing revenue
- Monorails have no real cost advantage compared to intermediate capacity metros
- Most importantly, a power failure for a monorail can have terrible consequences, as cranes need to be employed to remove trapped passengers, unlike intermediate capacity metros, where passengers can walk to the next station

On the other hand, some of the advantages of monorails are:
- Quick to build
- Cheap
- Monorails can accept sharp curves, down to as low as 50 metres (that said, light rail vehicles can accept 15 to 25 metre curves)
- The airspace needed for monorails is smaller than for light metros

Overall, one could easily say that monorails offer no real advantages over a light metro system, and have only disadvantages, the most important of which is the inability to get passengers off a train that breaks down. It would seem reasonable to recommend that monorail systems should only be used where light rail or an intermediate capacity metro is impossible, and this would generally be rare.

Maglevs

Perhaps one of the most interesting rail systems is a technology called the "Maglev". This has been in existence since the 80's and there is constant talk of the installation of new maglev systems. At the time of writing of this book only one commercial Maglev system is in operation, and this connects Pudong airport to the Shanghai metro system. A picture of this system is below:

Shanghai Maglev

Maglev is a contraction for magnetic levitation, and the train itself does not have any wheels and does not even contact the monorail. The train floats above the monorail and, as it has no contact with any surface, can reach speeds of over 400 kms/hr.

Despite the promise of Maglev technology, in practise only one commercial system has ever been installed. There also exists a low speed Maglev system in Japan, but its top speed is very low, so the full potential of the technology has not been achieved.

The author is not convinced by the arguments for a maglev train. The major problem to be overcome is economics, and central to this is the cost of accelerating trains to speeds over 400 kms/hr. A number of high speed trains have been developped, using conventional tracks, where speeds of over 350 kms/hr have been achieved. These trains rarely operate over 300 kms/hr as the power consumption required to drive trains at any speed faster than that is very high. Power consumption seems to increase exponentially with speed, and at 400 kms/hr power consumption must be very large indeed. This problem cannot really be resolved, other than constructing a vacuum tunnel for the maglev, something that seems rather improbable.

Tilt Trains

Tilt trains are an interesting type of technology used on intercity and regional services. The train tilts so that it can go around sharp curves at a higher speed. The speed increase can be considerable, and this technology, and the equations to calculate maximum speeds.

The greater the degree of tilt, the better the train can accept sharp curves. Tilt trains have revolutionised rail travel between many different centres, and can dramatically increase higher average speeds on existing rail lines, especially where those lines contain a lot of curves.

Tilt trains are normally only single deck, and passengers must be seated. The tilting action makes standing on a tilt train a little difficult.

The photo below is of a tilt train in Taiwan and from the outside it does not really appear any different to any other trains, although the outer shape is slightly different from other trains.

A Tilt Train in Taiwan

Tilting trains are usually regional or intercity trains, that travel from one city to another. It would be strange to use a tilt train within one large city, as a substitute for a metro or commuter system.

Tourist Trains

A tourist train is a train which provides an enjoyable experience to passengers, and may or may not connect important destinations that passengers may want to go. Most tourist railways go nowhere important, and the experience is the reason why the service is popular. Alternatively, a tourist railway may connect tourist destinations to the main rail system.

Tourist railways often use old rollingstock, which is custom made for that particular application. The structure of the rollingstock may be very unusual, and may not even afford protection from rain or wind. Some tourist railways connect hard to reach places, and the rollingstock required to achieve this can be very distinctive.

The picture below shows two different types of tourist tram in the town of Christchurch in New Zealand. On the left is the tourist tram that runs around the city, which is an old style tram that is rigid and very short. On the right is a tram that has been converted to be used as a restaurant.

Tourist Trams in Christchurch

Tourist railways can be divided into several categories:
- Railways through parklands, mountains, and other areas which are very scenic and the entire trip might last 1 to 2 hours. The Kuranda railway form Cairns in Australia up into the nearby mountains is probably the best known example of this type of train in Australia, but there are several others.
- Rail cruises, where the rail trip might take weeks, or in some cases, months. The cost of the ticket is extremely high, potentially thousands or tens of thousands of US dollars, for one ticket. Food is provided, and the quality can be very high. Passengers will sleep on the train. The Indian Pacific in Australia is an example of this type of rail service.
- Trains that are mostly "normal", but are richly decorated, and connect the rail system to an area which tourists commonly visit. The commuter train in Paris to the palace at Versailles is a good example of this kind of train, other examples include the Disneyland train in Hong Kong, or the Xinbeitou train in Taipei to the hots springs resorts. These trains are often visually impressive and richly appointed. There are no trains like this in Australia

- Old heritage trams that move throughout cities. These trams are often 100 years old, and have a lot of charm. The distance moved might be quite small. The best known example of this type of tram is the San Francisco heritage tram.
- Trains, that are more like trolleys, that climb steep inclines, and connect major destinations to carparks or other access points to a high value destination. This type of tourist railway is relatively common, and Perhaps the best known of these is the Peak Tram in Hong Kong, which connects the Peak on Hong Kong Island with the rest of the island. This type of tourist railway is sometimes used to connect mountains and ski fields to access points.
- Small railways, sometimes monorails, contained entirely in amusement parks, and are paid for an operated by the amusement park owner.

As can be seen from the list above, tourist railways are actually quite common and varied.

Tourist trains have high ticket prices, and so can operate at a profit. Passengers rarely would use a tourist railway for daily transportation.

REFERENCES

1. Zhang, Y & Yan, X & Comtois, C *Some Measures of Increasing Rail Transit Riderships: Case Studies*, Chinese Geographical Science, Volume 10, Number 1, pp 80 – 88, 2000

2. Smith K. *Alstom puts weight behind Citadis Dualis, International Railway Journal*, Feb 2010

3. ALSTOM, *AGV Full Speed Ahead into the 21st Century*, 2009, www.transport.alstom.com

4. BTS Group, *Annual Report 2009/2010* (the Bangkok Skytrain)

5. Kemp, R. *T618 – Traction Energy Metrics*, Rail Safety and Standards Board, Interfleet Technology, Dec 2007

6. Taipei Rapid Transit Corporation *2013 Annual Report*, http://english.metro.taipei/ct.asp?xItem=1056448&ctNode=70219&mp=1220 36

7. Dearien, J. *Ultralight Rail and Energy Use*, Encyclopaedia of Energy, Elsevier Publishing, March 2004

8. Siemens, *Siemens Velaro datasheet*, www.siemens.com/mobility

9. Fabian, J. *The Exceptional Service of Driverless Metros*, Journal of Advanced Transportation, Vol 33, No 1, pp 5-16

10. Kimijima, N. et al *New Urban Transport for Middle East Monorail System for Dubai Palm Jumeirah Transit System*, Hitachi Review Vol 59, (2010), No 1

11. IBI Group, E&N Railway Corridor Study: Analysis of Tourist Train Potential, (Date Unknown)

12. Hassan A The Role of Light Railway in Sugarcane Transport in Egypt, Infrastructure Design, Signalling and Security in Railway, Chapter 1

13. Parsons Brinkerhoff *High Speed Rail*, Network, Issue No 73, Sept 2011, http://www.pbworld.com/news/publications.aspx

14. Chun-Hwan, K. Transportation Revolution: The Korean High-speed Railway, Japan Railway & Transport Review 40, March 2005

15. Alstom Metropolis 21 st Century Metro Train Technology, http://www.alstom.com/turkey/products-and-services/-alstom-transport-turkey/rolling-stock/

16. Scomi Rail, *Monorail The Revolution of Urban Transit*, http://www.scomirail.com.my/

17. Duncan, B *The Hunter Rail Car: A versatile design solution for regional rail transport*, Australian Journal of Multi-disciplinary Engineering, Vol 7, No 2

18. Burge, P. et al Modelling Demand for Long-Distance Travel in Great Britain, www.rand.org, 2011

19. Railway Gazette *Commissioning the world's heaviest automated metro*, Metro Report 2003

20. Stadler *Electric Double-Deck train KISS*, www.stadlerrail.com

21. Transportation Research Board *Integration of Light Rail Transit into City Streets*, 1996

22. Turnbull, G. *The development and retention of Melbourne's trams and the influence of Sir Robert Risson*, ISSN 1038-7448, Working Paper No. 01/2002, Aug 2002

23. Transportation Research Board *Track Design Handbook for Light Rail Transit*, Second Edition, TCRP Report 155, 2012

24. Mora, J. *A Streetcar named Light Rail*, IEEE Spectrum Feb 1991

25. Sarunac, R. & Zeolla, N. *Structural and Crashworthiness Requirements of Light Rail Vehicles with Low-Floor Extension*, Transportation Research Circular E-C058: 9th National Light Rail Conference

26. Schroeder, M. *Developing CEM Design Standards to Improve Light Rail Vehicle Crashworthiness*, Proceedings of JRC2006 Joint Rail Conference April 2006 Atlanta

27. Daniel, L. *Light Rail Systems – Assessing Technical Feasibility*, Conference on Railway Engineering Melbourne May 2006

28. Swanson, J. & Thomes, C. *Light-Rail Transit Systems*, IEEE Vehicular Technology Magazine, June 2010

29. Transportation Research Board National Research Council *TCRP Report 2 Applicability of Low-Floor Light Rail Vehicles in North America*, 1995

30. Coifman, B. *IVHS protection at light rail grade crossings*, Proceedings of the 1995 IEEE/ASME Joint Railroad Conference, 1995

31. Swanson, J. *Light Rail Systems Without Wires*, Proceedings of the 2003 IEEE/ASME Joint Rail Conference April 2003

32. Maunsell Australia Pty Ltd, *Perth Light Rail Study*, 0284/05, August 2007

Chapter 4 Overview of Rail Infrastructure

Track

Track is the system that provides a running surface for rail wheels, and supports the rail vehicle. Track is easily one of the most important engineering systems for a railway, and is a central part of the design of any new rail system. Track is mostly standard in its design and configuration from many different railways, although there are some different types used for light rail systems.

Most rail systems use a fairly standard track system, with the exception of trams, monorails, and some light rail. For trams the rails are often embedded into the road, so as to allow road vehicles to pass over the rails as well as trams. Rails for trams have a separate and quite different design to normal rail. The shape of the rail, as well as the system by which the rail is held in place, is quite different.

Rails are made of steel. Some smaller rail systems run on concrete viaducts, but the vast majority of rail systems use steel rails. Train wheels are also often made of steel, and the behaviour of this steel to steel physical interface is very important. Surprisingly, the steel wheels of the train can often slide over the steel top surface, and when this happens the top of the rail and the wheel can be badly damaged. Care must be taken in ensuring that the wheel never slides over the rail, but rolls instead, and this requirement is central to the design of any rail system. One way to avoid this problem is to use rubber tyred trains, and this is occasionally done, such as the Montreal metro, but so doing adds a lot of cost as rubber tyres need to be constantly replaced as they wear.

Much of the track around the world is ballasted, which means the sleepers and rails sit on ballast. Ballast is made up of crushed rock, and major railways use substantial quantities of it. Sleepers sit within the ballast, and the ballast holds them in place. The major alternative to ballasted track is slab track, where the sleepers and rail sit directly on concrete. The track structure for ballasted track is shown below.

Figure 4.1 Track System

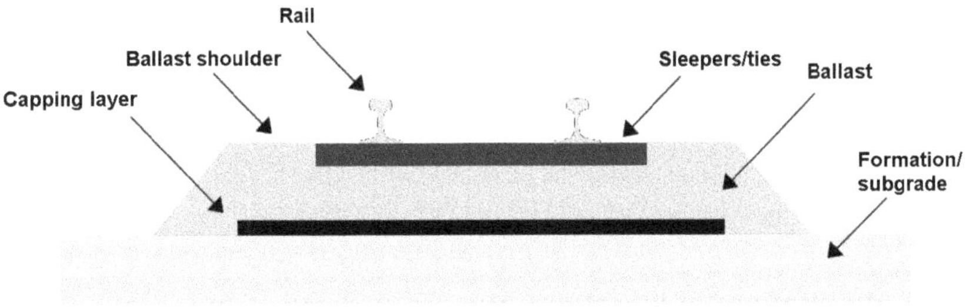

The function of each of the components of the track system is:

- The rail; supports the train, provides a running surface for the wheels of each train.
- Sleepers; which support the rails, hold the rails at a fixed distance from each other, and transfer the weight and load of the train into the ballast. Sleepers are often made of wood or concrete, although other materials such as steel or polymer are also used
- Ballast, which sits under the rails, and is made of hard crushed rock. Ballast distributes the load from trains, reducing wear, so that many trains can pass without causing serious damage to the track system. Ballast is a sacrificial item, which means it is designed to degrade over time. The degradation of ballast, and managing its replacement, is one of the key maintenance activities of any railway.
- The capping layer; which provides separation between the ballast and the subgrade. The capping layer maintains the separation between the ballast and the formation. The capping layer is sometimes replaced with geosynthetics, which is a type of textile matting, keeping the formation and ballast separate.
- Formation: which is usually the compacted ground underneath the track structure. The formation supports the track, and the condition of the formation is one of the key parameters for determining the maintenance of track.

Tracks are normally in pairs. Away from the track the ground normally has a fall to it, this is to allow for the water to run away from the track.

Figure 4.2 The Double Track System

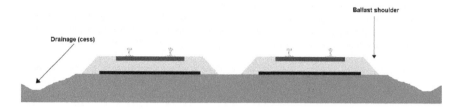

Drainage is very important for any track system. Drains need to be provided so that water can be removed when the track is rained on. Drainage, or the lack of it, can cause substantial problems in any rail system.

The rails are fastened to the sleepers with specially designed fasteners. The picture below shows the clips holding the rails to the sleepers.

Rail Track

If the reader looks carefully, notice that most of the rail is rusty, but on top of the rail there is part of it where train wheels sit when travelling over the rail. This patch of worn shiny rail is called the wear band, or the contact band, and it's important for a rail system to maintain this clear band of clean steel for signalling equipment to operate. The picture below shows it better.

Rail Fastenings

Rails are quite standard, and come in a number of sizes. Rail sizes are usually expressed in weight per unit of length, and in metric countries this is often 53 or 60 kgs per metre. Other sizes are also possible, with 40 and 50 also being common. In the large heavy haul freight networks in northern Australia, 74 kg/metre is now being used (as of 2012), which is a very large size and suitable for very heavily loaded trains with a high frequency. The imperial unit of measurement is pounds per yard, and 40 to 100 pounds per yard is common.

Increasing the size of the rail increases the size of train that can pass over the rails. For a light rail system, only a small rail is needed, and where small trains operate only small rails are needed. For larger trains, and especially freight lines, the rails need to be large to accommodate the higher weight.

Figure 4.3 The Rail Profile

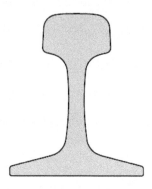

Above is a very standard profile for rails. The top is called the head of the rail. Different sizes of rail have slightly different shapes, but overall they mostly look similar to the rail shape above. Tram rails look significantly different, and monorails do not have rails, but just the one beam. The image below shows the profile of a tram rail, and it is designed to allow trains to run on it and allow road vehicles to drive over it as well.

Figure 4.4 Tram Rail Profile

The ballast underneath the track plays an important role. The main purpose of ballast is to maintain and support the track, which is generally is does well, but also to suppress vibration. Trains moving over tracks generate a lot of noise and vibration, and the ballast, surprisingly enough, suppresses this. Ballast is even used in tunnels, to suppress noise, again which is does quite well. It seems strange that ballast does this, but it does.

Ballast is made up of many small hard rocks. The amount of ballast placed under the track is not fixed, and more is usually better. Putting more ballast is expensive, as the stuff is unexpectedly expensive, and actually quite heavy. The best ballast if tough and rough, and locks together to form a tight bed for the sleepers and rails. Generally the harder the better, and quartz and granite are often considered the best materials, but many different types of rock are used. Railways often use materials that are found locally, to reduce costs and ensure the ballast does not need to be shipped very far.

Achieving the great noise reduction that ballast achieves is done through breaking down the ballast. Each time a train passes over the ballast, a small amount of it breaks into smaller pieces. Over a long period of time, such as decades, the ballast breaks down into such small pieces that most of it becomes powder. The powder intermixed with the rocky ballast is often described as fines. Once the ballast is full of fines it needs to be either cleaned, or entirely replaced, and both of these options are not cheap. Also, the track will be unable to hold track geometry, and this can be a real problem for high speed track where maintaining good track geometry is quite important.

So in summary ballast is a sacrificial item. This means that it is designed to be destroyed, which on most tracks it will be sooner or later. As ballast degrades, it gets smaller, and so the track starts to sink. Over a period of time the track can sink up to 200 mm, and if this occurs at a platform, train floors will be lower than the platform. For maintenance, railways often top up ballast as it degrades.

Ballast maintenance drives a very large part of the maintenance for a rail system. There is much to be said about what type of ballast to install, when to clean it, and when to replace it. These decisions are important for the maintenance of a rail system, and a good rail maintenance organisation will carefully consider how to make these decisions. For the purposes of rail transport planning, the choice of ballast, or even if it is to be used, can influence the way services are provided to customers. This very detailed and interesting topic is unfortunately a bit too long to be fully explained here; one of the many compromises needed to complete this book and not let it get too long. But to provide a very quick summary:

- Better quality ballast costs more, and degrades more slowly. Reducing the maintenance can sometimes mean spending more on the ballast when it is purchased
- Better quality ballast provides more track stability and the geometry degrades more slowly

- Providing more ballast when the track is installed, or deeper ballast, allows the load from trains to be spread more evenly and the ballast will degrade more slowly. An alternative is to use lighter trains, or a lower frequency of service
- The geometry requirements for high speed rail are very high, and so using ballast means that track geometry will need to be constantly checked

Below is a very simple illustration of how ballast degrades and its effect on track geometry. The diagram below looks at track side on, so we can see what happens when ballast degrades.

Figure 4.5 Track in Good Condition

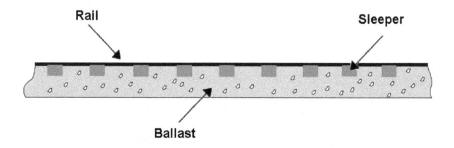

The track above is nice and flat and will provide a lovely smooth running surface for trains. Once the track has been used for a few years, and depending on a few things like the type of traffic, how much of it there is, and the amount of rainfall and the quality of the drainage, then the track will start to sink. When it sinks then it will start to look something like what is drawn below:

Figure 4.6 Degraded Track

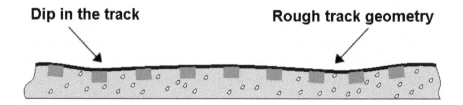

Again, the overall mechanics of track degradation have been heavily simplified here. There are a number of other track geometry parameters, and these also degrade, and need to be checked and measured by qualified maintenance personnel. Despite this, what is shown above is the most common cause of track geometry problems, and the one that usually determines much of the maintenance spending.

The degradation of ballast is a real problem for station design. It needs to be accounted for, and the track and rail position "moves around". This presents many problems, the most important of which, is that the platform gap needs to be increased in size. In some cases the platform gap is enormous, and this can be a real problem for people with disabilities.

The photo below is of tram tracks in Hong Kong that have been uncovered during maintenance work. Rarely is there any ballast for tram tracks, and as can be seen from the photo below the tracks are embedded into the road, and surrounded in bitumen. This type of systems does not allow the noise suppression that normally comes with using ballast, especially at joins, ie, where two rails are joined together.

Uncovered Tram Tracks in Hong Kong

So why is more slab track not used? Slab track, or putting the rails and sleepers onto concrete, seems to eliminate many of the problems associated with ballast. Ballast is expensive, and needs to be replaced after it has degraded. When it sinks it creates all sorts of track geometry problems, which can only be fixed with expensive track maintenance vehicles.

Slab track in Bangkok is shown below, on the Bangkok Skytrain. Note that on this track a third rail is also used, and it is located in between both running tracks.

Slab Track in Bangkok

Slab track is technically more complex to install. Problems with vibration usually mean that the concrete base can be damaged, and so vibration damping is needed. Whilst this function is normally provided by ballast, this is not possible with slab track, so some complicated vibration dampening scheme is needed. Different types of these have been designed and are in use, and quality control when they are installed is very important.

In some cases track may be designed for two gauges. Dual gauge track is sometimes needed in boundaries between areas with different gauges. Below is dual gauge track, this one is located in Brisbane, the inside rails are narrow gauge, and the outside are standard gauge. As Queensland uses narrow gauge, the inside rails are used more often than the outside ones.

Double Gauge Track

Signalling

The signalling system plays a critical role in any railway. Train movements are constrained by the signalling system. Trains are not like cars where they can travel along, and then stop when reaching an intersection. Almost all railways (excluding trams and light rail) operate on the principle that all rail tracks are divided up into sections, or blocks, and to enter each section trains need authorisation. For the most part trains are authorised to enter track sections using signals.

The signalling system is more than just signals, although this is the most obvious part of the signalling system. The purpose of the signalling system is to authorise the movement of trains, communicate this to drivers, and to keep trains separate so that one does not collide with another. The signalling system is composed of many different parts, including:
- Signals
- Track circuits and axle counters (train detection)
- Points installed over turnouts
- Signal boxes, and the control panel that display where trains are
- Interlockings

Signalling, like track design and the design of electrical power systems, is a huge area that has specialist people working in for decades, and there are courses and textbooks written on this asset system. Again, it is not possible here to provide anything but the simplest explanation of how this system operates.

Signals provide information to drivers of trains; the driver sees the signal, and then knows what to do. The driver has control over the motor of the train, and the brakes, and can instruct the motor to drive harder, or slower, or brake the train. He/she does this in response to what the signal displays. The driver almost always cannot determine the direction of the train, and so his control of the train is limited to setting the speed.

Some signalling systems do not have signals by the side of the track, but instead replicate signals in the driver's cabin. The driver can see the relevant indications on his control panel, and this is called "in-cab signalling". This style of signalling system is becoming more and more common, as it eliminates the need for lineside signalling, which is expensive to install and maintain. For the purposes of explaining how the signalling system works, it is helpful to examine how lineside signals work, as this can effectively explain how signals control the movement of trains.

The purpose of the signalling system is to prevent trains colliding with each other, as well as managing the passage of trains through the rail system. Trains stop by braking, and this means that the wheels use the rail to stop the train. As trains have steel wheels, and the rails are made of steel, then trains need to stop by braking through their wheels onto the rail. Steel normally slides quite well over steel, so trains need to stop slowly, and a typical trains moving at 70 kms/hr might need 500 metres to stop. Trains moving at higher speeds may need greater distances to stop, and the signalling system needs to inform the driver well ahead of time that there is a stop signal ahead, and then the train needs to be slowed so that it can stop.

Many rail systems require the signalling system to provide something called a "movement authority". This is the permission to move through a rail system, and to perform any movement. Many signalling systems grant movement authority for trains to move, often through the use of signals. More advanced signalling systems also use movement authorities.

Light rail and trams often use road signals for movement authorities. Trams may use traffic signals like road vehicles, although sometimes they have rail like signals that direct their movements. Signals on light rail and trams systems, where they exist, tend to be very simple. Light rail and trams also run on steel rails, and have steel wheels, so their ability to stop will be similar to that of any other rail vehicle. The steel on steel sliding problem, mentioned above, applies equally to trams and light rail vehicles but trams do not move very fast, and so can slow down in time to stop at red traffic lights. Modern light rail vehicles are equipped with magnets that latch onto the rail and provide additional deceleration. It's this new braking system that allows light rail vehicles to brake hard, and so use traffic lights as signals.

What colours are used on the signals, and how the lights are arranged, varies substantially from railway to railway, and from country to country. There is very little standardisation between countries, even within the same country. Even in Australia, which has only a rail system moderate in size, the style and structure of signals varies from railway to railway. This makes explaining signalling in a book of this type extremely difficult, as it's impossible to explain all the different scenarios, the US is different to French signalling, and so on. The method used here is to use NSW signalling, as the author is familiar with it, and it looks like traffic lights, so it's a bit easier to explain. Again, this situation is a difficult one, and there is no real best answer as to how to explain signalling systems in general.

The picture below is of a signal is the Sydney rail system. This one has two red lights illuminated, with a black background. This signal is described as a double light signal, as there are basically two signals, one of top of the other. The use of two heads for a signal allows the provision of additional information.

A Double Light Signal

The signalling system was designed to give drivers the warning time they need to stop the train, otherwise a collision could result. The most common way to do this is to put "signals" alongside the track to tell the driver what to do. As the driver drives his train he sees the signals, and based on what colours are displayed he knows what to do. It is the signalling system that determines the number of trains that can pass through a section per hour, and this is called the train frequency. The minimum time between trains is another important measure, and this is called the headway.

So who controls the signals? Signals can display many different meanings, and there needs to be some sort of decision making process to determine what is displayed. For road traffic lights many of these are controlled by computer, or sometimes by controllers at a control centre somewhere. Rail signals can be computer controlled, and many are, but many are also controlled by a person with a job description of "signaller", or in the USA and Canada a "dispatcher". The signaller sets the signals, and so controls the movements of trains. Signallers are physically located in signal boxes.

Signalling systems around the world can be divided into two broad categories; speed signalling, where the driver of the train is told the maximum permitted speed, and route signalling, where the driver is told the direction he will go, and not the actual speed. It might seem strange that the driver may not know where he is going, but in complex junction there might be many points lying in many different directions, and it may not be clear to him which track is the one that he will take. In a complex junction there may be ten or even more different possible directions, and the driver will need to know which one his train will take. Of course almost always the driver is not free to choose the path his train will take, but will need to follow the path chosen for him by the signaller.

Below are some lights and signals for the trams system in Hong Kong. At this turnout trams can go either to the left or the right, and the traffic light shows either a white line perpendicular up, or sloping to the left. This traffic light is operating as a route indicator. Trams can possible go two ways, to the left and right, to the tram stop ahead. The traffic light gives the tram permission to proceed, and in the middle of the picture is the route indicator, that displays how the points are set, so the tram driver knows where the tram will go. Route indicators such as the one below are more common in rail systems in commonwealth countries.

Hong Kong Route Indicator

There is absolutely no standard for signalling systems around the world. There are a very large number of different ways of constructing signalling systems, and signals can vary even within the same country. The enormous variety of different ways of building signalling systems makes it difficult in a book like this one to explain how this kind of system works, and it is necessary to find a common thread between the many different signalling systems. An attempt has been made below to do this, but the reader must remember that is impossible to explain anything more than the very basics of a signalling system.

What is described below is the British method of signalling. It is used in most of Australia, and places like Hong Kong and Singapore. It is obviously also used in the UK. The structure of the signalling is common to many countries, and has the basic rule of red/yellow/green, also used for traffic lights. This basic structure is also used in France and the US, but this is really the only commonality. For this reason these basic signals are described, and nothing more complex than this is explained.

The driver of a train needs to know the speed he should drive the train at. In speed signalling the driver is told the speed, but for route signalling a speed is not explicitly displayed. For route signalling the driver needs to have extensive route knowledge, and need to know the speed for different areas and different signal indications. This, for a large system, can be a lot of knowledge, and it may take years to train a driver to know all of the speeds in all of the different locations. Even in a route signalled railway (such as the rail system in Sydney) there is usually some information on speeds, and speed signs telling the driver his maximum speed are common. Information on speeds however is not complete, and for any speed other than a full proceed indication it may not be clear what speed the driver of a train should go, and experience will be his guide. To the casual reader this might seem pretty crazy, but in practice it is possible to successfully run a railway where the speeds in many situations are known only by experience.

The schematic below shows a very basic signal. The top part of the signal is called the signal head, and signals may have one or more of these. There are lights installed in the head of the signal, and there may be only one, or multiple of these. Remember that many railways do no structure their signal this way, but some do, and for the purposes of explaining how signalling works, this signal design is clear and easy to understand.

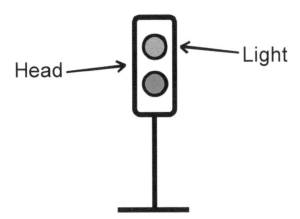

Notice that the green is on top, and the red is below the green. Whilst this is not always how signals are structured, this layout seems to be common. Normally only one signal light would be lit at any one time.

The "*aspect*" of a signal is its appearance, so if the green light is on we say that the signal is showing a green aspect. The "*indication*" of the signal is the meaning of the signal to the driver, and for a green aspect this will be a proceed indication.

So what do the colours mean? Well green means "Proceed", which is go at full line speed, at the place where the rail signal is located. The red means "Stop", which obviously means stop. These two colours are the minimum for any signal that can display different indications, but a signal can also be a single red light. Many more different meanings can be created, and some of these are discussed below.

Whilst in principle the signalling system is simple, in practice it is a bit more complicated than that. The interpretation of the signals can get quite complicated, especially in freight yards, and where there are many possible different routes. It can get even more complicated where there are level crossings and marshalling yards next to each other. A full discussion of what signals can display and what the meaning is far outside the scope of this book.

In practice the use of a two light signal has serious limitations, and so it is often not used, despite its simplicity. The table below shows a three light single headed signal, and the relevant indications. This type of signal is very common.

3 Aspect/Light Signals with Indications (Example)

Signal	Indication (meaning)
	Proceed, travel at full line speed to at least until the next signal can be seen. This signal is called "**Clear**" in the US.
	Caution, be prepared to stop at the signal in advance of this one. Drivers seeing this signal would reduce speed. This signal is called "**Approach**" in the US.
	STOP, do not drive any further than this signal. This signal is also called "Stop" in the US.

There are many other possible indications that can be created, such as for shunting moves, but these are not discussed any further.

The use of the three colours, red, green and yellow is very common. Where signals need to display additional information, then some more lights of the same colour may be added, or one of the lights may flash to provide a different indication. In the US there was a fourth colour, lunar white, which is a blueish white.

Where four indications are required to control the speed, then sometimes a fourth indication is used. In the US this signal is called "*Advance Approach*", and in Australia the name "*medium*" is commonly used. This indication is used to tell drivers that, 2 signals in front the current signal, that this signal is at stop.

A Fourth Indication	
Signal	**Indication (meaning)**
	Medium, driver should be aware that the second signal after this signal is at stop, and to be prepared to stop at that signal. Called "Advance Approach" in the US. To provide this indication, sometimes, the yellow light will flash, with no other lamp lit.

With speed signalling, the signalling system tells the driver the speeds, and for the US, the table below provides a rough guide as to what speeds are common. These names are

US Speed Signalling Speeds and Names	
Indication	**Speed (approx)**
Normal (full proceed)	Line speed (which depends on the

	location)
Limited	40 – 45 miles per hour (about 60 kms/hr)
Medium	30 miles per hour (about 45 kms/hr)
Low	15 miles per hour (about 20-25 kms/hr)
Restricted	15 miles per hour or less, and the driver should be prepared to stop quickly

The relationship between the signal indication and the most desirable speed the driver should drive at can be a bit complicated.

The signalling system includes more than just the signals that control the actions of train drivers. Another important component of the signalling system is the method of detecting the presence and location of trains, and this is commonly done with two pieces of engineering equipment; the track circuit and the axle counter. These items are able to sense when trains enter and exit fixed blocks of track, and provide this information back to the signalling system. The signalling system uses this information to make decisions about what signals should display, as well as provide this information to the signaller.

The heart of all signalling systems is the interlocking. An interlocking is the key device that prevents trains from running into another. In a junction, or a crossover, one trains passes in front of another, and it is possible for the two trains to collide. The interlocking checks that there are no trains in the way when a train is sent through a crossover or a junction. The interlocking takes information from the train detection system and makes some calculations, and then decides if trains can be allowed through junctions. Interlockings are very safety critical, and they must be designed with great care to ensure that there is no possibility that trains will collide with each other.

Signals are very important to calculating the capacity or headway of a rail system. This topic is extremely important for calculating how many people can be moved by a rail system.

Electrical (Traction systems)

Electrical power is often supplied to power them. Electricity is generated at a power station, or possibly locally and closer to the railway, and is then transmitted through transmission lines, to the railway. Once the power has reached the railway it is transformed down to the appropriate voltage, and then delivered to the trains.

Connecting an electricity network all this distance is expensive, and there needs to be a good reason to build the infrastructure that allows this to happen. Whilst it is true that the emissions from electrical power is mostly lower than from diesel locomotives, there are other reasons why electric power is preferred over diesel engines. These include:

- Electric trains are quieter than diesel trains
- Electric energy is much cheaper than diesel fuel
- Diesel engines produce a lot of smoke from combustion, and in tunnels the smoke is quite unpleasant for passengers
- Diesel engines require fuel, which in certain circumstances can ignite, and this is a fire risk which requires additional mitigations in tunnels
- And as mentioned previously, normally CO_2 emissions are higher from diesel fuel than from electrical energy supplied from a generator
- For high speed trains diesel trains are limited on the top speed to 250 kms/hr, which is too slow for many high speed rail services

Almost all rail services in major cities are electric, although there are some exceptions. Freight services are mostly diesel, although as with many things in rail, there are some more exceptions. In Australia the Mount Black railway line is entirely electrified, and very large amounts of coal are moved on that rail line, so it certainly is possible to electrify freight lines.

There are two main ways to supply power to a train, using overhead wiring, or a third rail. Overhead wiring is generally preferred, although it makes the rail line look messy. For overhead wiring the wires hang down from above the train, and then the train has a matching system that allows it to reach up and touch the wires. This part of the train is called the pantograph. As a general observation, overhead wiring is preferred as the live electrical wires are far above the track, so that track workers can walk along the track without the need to isolate power. Also trespassers are not in any danger when entering the rail corridor as the wires are too high.

The alternative to overhead wiring is a third rail system. Third rail systems are often used because they are cheap to install, and tunnels with third rail systems are smaller and so are cheaper. Many urban rail systems have third rails installed. One challenge with third rails is that anyone that touches them will be instantly killed, and they are at ground level and so easy to reach.

The schematic below shows how overhead wiring is often configured.

Figure 4.7 Overhead Wiring and Structure

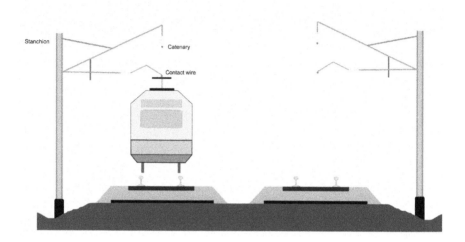

Overhead wiring needs to be supported and usually strong beams are concreted into the ground to hold the entire structure up. These beams in Australia are called stanchions, and are visually unappealing. Rail lines with no electric power are definitely visually more appealing than those with electric power. Recently there have been attempts to smarten up the appearance of rail lines with overhead wiring, with colours that are similar to the colours of the surroundings, with some success.

Overhead wiring structures come in many different shapes and sizes. The one below is for 25 kV, and is bolted onto a tunnel wall.

Registration and Contact Wire Support

Below is a pantograph that conducts electricity from the contact wire into the traction systems in the train. The top of the pantograph has a strip of carbon, and this wears as it rubs along the contact wire. The pantograph is pushed up hard against the contact wire with springs, and so if the contact wire is removed then the pantograph will spring up high into the air.

A Pantograph

Below is a substation in Perth for converting power. A substation is a truly ugly thing, but it is needed to convert and use the power successfully.

Substations also contain electrical power equipment, much of which is fatal to the touch. Preventing trespassers from coming into contact with any of the equipment in a substation is a key requirement.

A Substation

The photo below shows a number of third rails in and around a couple of crossovers. Trains need to maintain contact with the third rail, and if contact is lost then the train will come to a stop, not immediately, but relatively quickly. Notice how much cleaner and nicer the track looks, and the appearance of the tracks is really much better.

Ballasted Track in a Viaduct with Third Rails

Installing power onto railways comes with many problems. Electricity in a DC (Direct Current) system can leak away, and if the leak is large enough, passengers or the public can be injured or even killed. The leaking electricity can do damage through a chemical process called electrolysis, which can result in metals near to the track being reduced to a soup of unpleasant chemicals.

For AC powered systems, there are other different problems to a DC system. The power moving through the overhead can induce currents in nearby metal objects, which means that there is now electricity in something that should not have it. For example, pipes along a tunnel in a system with AC power can now have currents passing through them. Again, this problem needs to be managed, and specialist technical people are needed who understand the problem.

A problem often encountered in Australia is that providing power to rail lines requires high voltage power lines running from generators to the rail line. In Australia generators are often located in remote areas next to coal supplies, and transmission lines need to run through national parks. Providing maintenance to transmission lines is raises some issues, as trees may need to be cut down. This is especially difficult where the trees are protected or endangered. Running power lines through a national park is a real problem, as access roads will need to be cut, and no one wants to do that. Even for a very conscientious and diligent railway, managing transmission lines through environmentally sensitive areas is difficult and constant problems emerge.

Overall providing electrical power to trains can be quite technically complicated. Specialist technical people are needed, and their salaries are not low. From the perspective of rail system design, only when the case for electric power is clearly overwhelming should electric power be used. Electric power provides many benefits and is the correct solution in many cases.

Railways in the past often generated their own power, and owned power stations. In Sydney the railways owned White Bay power station, as well as the Ultimo Power Station, which was effectively the first power station in Sydney. Rail systems in Australia now rarely own any form of power generation, and this is not changing. There has been a trend in Australia in the past 10 years to move power generation back closer to cities, and this is sometimes referred to as distributed power. There is much to be said about the case for railways having some form of power generation, especially in countries where power is very expensive to purchase. The author is of the opinion that a railway possessing some form of power generation is not necessarily a bad thing.

Tunnels

Tunnels provide many benefits, the main one being the ability of a rail line to avoid obstructions and other immovable objects, and still provide a transport service. Tunnels require large amounts of specialised infrastructure, and so are costly to construct and maintain. No discussion of rail infrastructure would be complete without a discussion of tunnels.

Tunnelling is a challenging area of engineering. The soil conditions are important to the costs and challenges associated with tunnelling, and there is no real way to know what the soil conditions will be like without actually tunnelling. To get an appreciation of the ground conditions, a project may organise for test bores to be drilled to sample what the ground is like, and this will provide some information on what the ground conditions are like. Whilst test bores provide some information, the actual ground conditions won't be known until digging actually commences.

Tunnels, and the management of fire in a tunnel, will impact upon station design. A "standard" tunnel will have ventilation, although many do not. All the ventilation equipment will normally be located at a station. An underground station can have a large amount of equipment, located in several large rooms within the station, including ventilation. The need to ventilate a tunnel significantly adds to the cost of constructing an underground station.

The picture below shows a rail tunnel, with the photo taken from one end of an underground station. Rail tunnels are commonly black or very dark with not much lighting. In this case this tunnel is single bore, and the track is ballasted, rather that being slab track. Note that the lighting is very close to the floor of the tunnel, so that drivers won't experience flashing lights when passing them, something that in rare instances can cause epileptic seizures.

A Tunnel and Portal

Whilst underground stations are also strictly speaking tunnels, they are not referred to as such, and the tunnels connect two underground stations. The transition from station to tunnel is shown below, with the station being light coloured and well-lit, and the tunnel dark and black. The transition from station into a tunnel is called a portal.

Rail tunnels can be described in terms of the following:
- The length of the tunnel
- What type of traffic is permitted to move through the tunnel
- The diameter of the tunnel, or if not round, the cross-sectional area
- The type of ventilation
- If the tunnel is single bore or double bore, and the configuration.

So let's discuss each of these in turn.

The length of the tunnel is probably the most important parameter for any rail tunnel. Usually measured in metres, it is measured as a distance that a person following the rail track would walk, rather than a linear distance from one portal to another. A long tunnel would be over 1 km in length, although there are many tunnels over 10kms, these are a small percentage of the total number of tunnels worldwide. In the US tunnels less than 160 metres are not described as tunnels, and are not normally classified as tunnels (at least under NFPA 130).

Most rail tunnels have passenger traffic moving through them. The composition of the rail traffic is quite important for a rail tunnel, but a casual observer would probably not be able to tell from looking at the tunnel what type of traffic was using the tunnel. Putting either diesel freight or passenger trains through the tunnel may change the equipment installed into it, or maybe not. Most freight trains are diesel powered, and this fuel is carried on board the train, and fuel leaks and fires are possible. Diesel engines can also catch fire, and this is particularly the case with older or more poorly maintained locomotives. Diesel locomotives dramatically increase the risk in a tunnel, and typically are excluded from tunnels used by passenger trains.

The risk and challenge with rail tunnels is fires. As tunnels are confined spaces, any fires can quickly incapacitate any passengers in the train. The heat itself is not the danger, but the smoke produced from the fire. Small fires are often started through vandalism in trains, but large fires are rare. The hazard of a large fire has a very low probability of occurrence, but when they occur the number of deaths can be very large. Preventing fires, or providing some method of escape for a tunnel can greatly add to the cost of the construction of a rail.

The diameter of the tunnel is an important parameter. Most tunnels are roughly circular in shape, so it's possible to customary the cross-sectional area of the tunnel from the diameter, using the very simple formula $Area = \dfrac{\pi D^2}{4}$. A typical diameter for a rail tunnel is about 7 metres, and a typical cross-sectional area about 40 to 60 metres. Larger cross sectional areas make ventilation and management of the movement of air in the tunnel easier, and overall a larger tunnel is better than a smaller one. Trains need to push the air out of the way when moving through a tunnel, and where there is little room between the walls of the tunnel and the train then the power needed to move the train is significantly greater. Also very narrow tunnels will make the air hotter as trains pass through, and the heat can become very great.

The type of ventilation is also relevant, and there are a number of different types. Many tunnels have no ventilation at all, but for new tunnels ventilation is often installed. Ventilation is required based on the length of the tunnel, the frequency of traffic, and the cross-sectional area of the tunnel. Ventilation can be described as either transverse, or longitudinal. For transverse ventilation, air is pushed into the tunnel from the walls towards the middle of the tunnel, whereas longitudinal the air is pushed in from the end of the tunnel, from one end to another.

And the final part of describing a rail tunnel is its configuration, and it can be single or twin bore. The table below lists many of the different configurations possible for a rail tunnel.

Different Tunnel Configurations

Tunnel Type	Comment
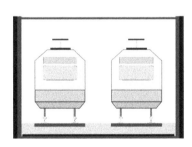	This is a single cut and cover tunnel. Cut and cover tunnels often have straight sides, unlike the curved sides of the other tunnels below. As cut and cover tunnels are often close to the surface, tunnels can be naturally ventilated.
	This is a tunnel with two tracks, in a single bore tunnel. There is no separate tunnel for escape or for service vehicles. The shape of the upper tunnel is often described as a horseshoe.

Different Tunnel Configurations

Tunnel Type	Comment
	A tunnel with two tracks, with a circular tunnel. There is no separate escape nor service tunnel. This type of tunnel is common for deep tunnels..
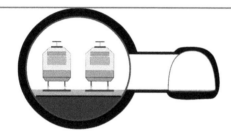	A circular rail tunnel with a supporting rail passage. This configuration is helpful if the need arises for an escape from the tunnel, and getting maintenance staff to equipment in the tunnel. The additional tunnel is expensive to construct.
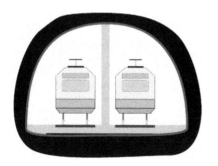	A horseshoe shaped tunnel, with a large concrete wall down the middle. The tunnel is split into two sections, which allows passengers to escape should the need arise down one of the two tunnels. This tunnel construction is commonly used in Hong Kong, and is relatively cheap.
	A double bore tunnel with cross-passages between each of the

Different Tunnel Configurations

Tunnel Type	Comment
	tunnels. This kind of configuration is common for long tunnels and those that carry freight.

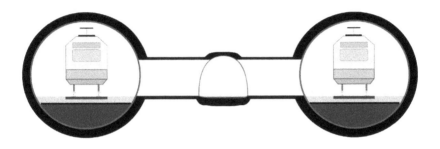

A double bore tunnel with a service tunnel in the middle, with cross passages. This is the configuration used on the Chunnel between England and France. This configuration is a very good one, and convenient for maintenance and escape from fires. Unfortunately it's really expensive.

Below is the layout of a twin bore tunnel in plan view. The key features are shown.

Figure 4.7 Rail Track through Tunnels

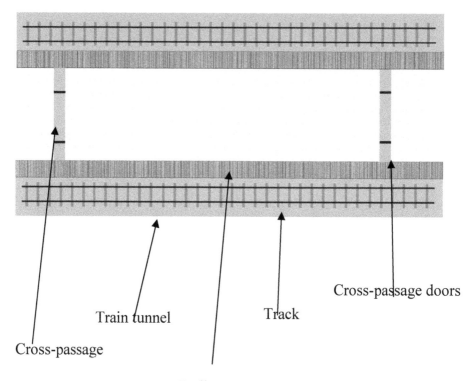

Cross-passage doors

Train tunnel   Track

Cross-passage

Walkway

The main components of this tunnel system are:
1/ the tunnels
2/ the tracks
3/ the walkway next to the tracks
4/ the cross-passages
5/ the doors in the cross-passages.

We note that rail tunnels are with the two tracks side by side are normally built with side platforms, and those with twin tunnels are island platforms. Will this rule does not need to always be followed, it often is.

Bridges

Everyone knows what bridges are and what they do. Any large rail system will have dozens, if not hundreds of bridges. Bridges are used to get the rail system across natural obstacles such as rivers, roads, valleys, and other natural obstacles.

Bridges are an attractive asset for any rail system. They are usually low maintenance, and they rarely contain any moving parts. In some cases rail lines pass over draw or swing bridge, but generally this is uncommon. The Skelton viaduct in Yorkshire is one rare example of a rail system using a swing bridge, and the El Ferdan bridge in Egypt over the Nile is another.

Bridges need to be very strong, but constructed properly they are can last hundreds of years. The one below is over the Cooks River in Sydney.

A Rail Bridge

Bridges that move, such as swing bridges and drawbridges, have some safety issues. There have been a number of fatal accidents in the US on swing bridges. Bridges that need to be opened and closed can be a problem, and these are usually situated over bodies of water, and are installed to allow large boats to pass underneath them. Care needs to be taken that the train does not enter over the bridge when it is open, otherwise the train can plunge into the water, and that's not good.

One problem with rail bridges, especially where the railway passes over a highway, is that occasionally trucks with high loads will strike the bridge. When this happens care must be taken that the bridge has not been damaged, and sometimes it is damaged, and trains need to slowly pass over the bridge just in case it has suffered some damage. Raising rail bridges is an important part of investing into rail infrastructure, as the higher the bridge over the highway, the smaller the chance that there will be a collision. Where a truck does hit a bridge, it can make a terrible mess and the damage to the truck can be considerable.

A more complicated version of a bridge is a viaduct. A viaduct is a long section of bridges that are all connected together. Viaducts are often used over marshy or swampy terrain, or for high speed rail.

The Viaduct connecting Italy with Venice

The picture above is of the viaduct that connects Venice to mainland Italy. This viaduct is needed because the ocean separates the historical city from Italy, and so the viaduct is quite long.

Road and Pedestrian Level Crossings

Level crossings are places where road vehicles are able to cross rail tracks. The picture below shows a level crossing outside of Paris, and it has lights and bells installed. Level crossings are sometimes described as being an "at-grade" crossing.

A Level Crossing in Paris

Level crossings can have a boom or booms installed, which descends when a train is approaching the level crossing. The boom provides an additional visual aid to drivers that the road level crossing is alarming, and that a train is coming.

Level crossings are installed in huge numbers around the world. The majority of level crossings in Australia do not have any form of protection or warning system installed over them, and they are just a place where road vehicles can cross the track. Many level crossings only have lights and bells and no boom.

Level crossings can pose some serious risks to trains and users. Every year there are fatal accidents at level crossings, and people are killed. In almost all cases the driver of the road vehicle has crossed the level crossing without looking, and there has been a collision. There have also been accidents involving buses and can result in the deaths of dozens of people.

Level crossings are places of high risk for any rail system. The construction of bridges is a viable alternative, and bridges pose almost no safety risk to trains. The cost of bridges is not small, and replacing hundreds of level crossings with bridges is simply not possible for many railways operating on limited budgets.

Tram systems operate at road level, and so effectively the entire system is one giant level crossing. There are rarely fatal accidents involving trams, as the operational speed is rather low, and the drivers know to look out for cars. Low speed collisions between road vehicles and trams are however very common, and in one year there were over one thousand collisions such as this in Melbourne. Fatal accidents with trains seem to occur when the train is moving fairly fast, and the impact to the road vehicle has the energy to cause substantial mechanical damage.

Level crossings can be a part of the signalling system, because if the level crossing has bells and lights then the signalling system needs to tell the level crossing when to activate. A level crossing with no protection other than a sign has no connection to the signalling system. Complex level crossings can be expensive to maintain.

Papers have been written in the US where the benefits of installing lights, bells and booms has been analysed. The US has an extraordinary high number of deaths at level crossings, typically over 300 per year, a figure that would not be accepted in almost any other country in the world. The US government has had a long term plan to close, remove, or install lights and booms over as many level crossings as possible, and this program has been very successful in reducing the number of deaths per year. It is clear that booms work quite well in reducing the number of deaths at level crossings.

Another significant problem with level crossings is making sure that the lights and bells don't ring for too long. Car drivers quickly get bored waiting at level crossings, and they are tempted to drive around the boom after waiting even a short period of time like 1 or 2 minutes. Many of the accidents have occurred this way in the world over level crossings. In practice signalling systems have difficulties in allowing for the different speeds of trains, and so for a slow moving train the lights and bells may flash and ring for a time period much longer than a couple of minutes.

Sometimes there are pedestrian level crossings attached to road crossings. A pedestrian crossing is designed purely for passengers, and it operates in a very similar way to a road crossing. Pedestrian crossings are much smaller than road crossings, and have lights and booms. Pedestrian crossings in Australia at least are less common than road crossings.

There are also other types of rail crossings, but they are fairly unusual. There are sometimes crossings provided for animals, and in Sydney there is a horse crossing next to Rosehill Racecourse. Crossings for animals needs to be designed differently than for people, and more space needs to be provided, depending on the size of the animal. Given the rarity of level crossings designed for animals, they won't be discussed any further.

Control Systems

A control system for a railway is an engineering system that displays the position of trains and the status of signals. Control systems normally have a computer screen where trains and their position are displayed. Large rail systems have particularly large control system displays, and these can cover the wall of a large room.

Control systems display tracks as divided up into sections, and each section is displayed as either empty or occupied. Trains are often identified with some sort of alphanumeric code, such as 111A, which identified which run it is. Alternatively, the set number (ie the train identifier) can be displayed.

Control systems also allow the signaller to set trains to routes. This means that the signaller can set the direction of turnouts, and can direct the movement of trains. Remember that drivers mostly cannot set turnout directions themselves (although there are exceptions to this rule, once again), and this function is performed either by the signaller, or in modern times, a computer program.

Tram systems and light rail systems can also have control systems, but they operate differently, partly because of the simpler network design. There is often no track detection system for trams, or almost never, so trams need to be detected and found using a different system. GPS, or some system that effectively operates the same as GPS, can be used to locate where the trams are. On the control system the screen will show the location of the trams, but unlike a control system the trams can't be directed with points and track infrastructure to different routes. The control system for a tram system is much more passive.

A control system links in closely with the signalling system, but is not the same thing. The purpose of the signalling system is to prevent the collision of trains, and the purpose of control systems is to manage the movement of trains. If the control system is directed to allow two trains to collide with one another, then the signalling system will prevent it and send an alarm to the control system.

It is also common to refer to other systems that manage rail infrastructure as control systems. For example, a system that displays information on lifts and escalators may be called a control system. It is important to distinguish between the train control system, and a system that manages other rail infrastructure.

REFERENCES

1. Zhang, C. & Li, L. Zhang, D. & Zhang, S. *Types and Characteristics of Safety Accidents Induced by Metro Construction*, 2009 International Conference on Information Management, Innovation Management and Industrial Engineering, 209

2. Kimijima, N. et al *New Urban Transport for Middle East Monorail System for Dubai Palm Jumeirah Transit System*, Hitachi Review Vol 59, (2010), No 1

3. Murphy, E. *The Application of ERTMS/ETCS Systems*, IRSE Technical Convention Melbourne, Oct 2007

4. State of Florida Department of Transportation, *Central Florida Commuter Rail Transit Design Criteria*, October 2008

5. DB Netze *AG Network Statement 2014,* April 2013

6. Parsons Brinkerhoff *High Speed Rail*, Network, Issue No 73, Sept 2011, http://www.pbworld.com/news/publications.aspx

7. Lindahl, M. *Track geometry for high-speed railways*, Department of Vehicle Engineering Royal Institute of Technology, Stockholm 2001

8. Oura, Y. *Railway Electric Power Feeding Systems*, Japan Railway & Transport Review 16, June 1998

9. BSL Management Consultants *The Cost of Railway Infrastructure Status-Quo and Ways Ahead*, Presentation to the ProMain Council of Decision Makers, Brussels Nov 2001

10. Tateishi, Y. *Broadband Radio Transmissions in Railways*, JR EAST Technical Review-No 20

11. Zhang, W. et al *Pantograph and catenary system with double pantographs for high-speed trains at 350 km/hr or higher*, Journal of Modern Transportation, Volume 19, Number 1, March 2011

12. Eyre, P. *Signalling of the Southern Suburbs Railway*, IRSE Technical Convention – Perth, July 2007

13. Rail Industry Safety and Standards Board, *ROA Manual Section 01 Civil*

14. Kohel, J. *Optimised catenary maintenance measures on Austrian Federal Railways, Rail Engineering International Edition*, 2002 Number 1

15. Huth, P. *Overview of QR Signalling Principles*, IRSE Technical Meeting, Brisbane, July 2008

16. Kerr, D. Rail Signal Aspects and Indications, http://dougkerr.net/Pumpkin/articles/Rail_signal_aspects.pdf

17. Broderick, E. & Lemon, S. *Case Study: Application of CBTC on DLR*, IRSE   Australasia Technical Meeting, March 2011

18. Thales *SelTrac CBTC Communications-Based Train Control for Urban Rail*, www.thalesgroup.com/security-services

19. Siemens Transportation Systems *GSM-R Terminals Flexible GSM-R Dispatcher Systems, Terminals and Cab Radio Solutions*, http://www.siemens.com.au/files/Mobility/RI/Documents/mob_gsm-r_terminals.pdf

20. Railway Gazette *Commissioning the world's heaviest automated metro*, Metro Report 2003

21. Thales *Netrac 6613 Aramis*, www.thalesgroup.com

22. Victorian Rail Industry Operators Group Standards Track Circuit Types Characteristics and Applications, Nov 2009 http://ptv.vic.gov.au/assets/PTV/PTV%20docs/VRIOGS/VRIOGS-012.7.4-RevA.pdf

23. Davey, E. *Rail Traffic Management Systems, IET Railway Signalling and Control Systems Course*, May 2012

24. Ancarani, G. et al *Mobile radio for Railway Networks in Europe*, June 1999

25. Hillenbrand, W. *GSM-R The Railways Integrated Mobile Communications System*, Dec 1999, http://www.tsd.org/

26. Mok, S. & Savage, I. *Why Has Safety Improved at Rail-Highway Grade Crossings?*, Risk Analysis, Vol 25, No 4, 2005

27. Klinger, R. *Radio Coverage for Road and Rail Tunnels in Tunnels in the Frequency Range 75 to 1000 MHz*, Vehicular Technology Conference, 1991.

28. Ahren, T. & Parida, A. *Overall railway infrastructure effectiveness (ORIE)*, Journal of Quality in Maintenance Engineering Vol 15 No 1 2009, pp 17 – 30

Chapter 5 Stations

Stations are what passengers see when entering and leaving a rail system. They are an important place for passengers, and play a large role in the perceived success or failure of a rail system. Stations also have a large amount of infrastructure, and the trend with modern stations is to provide more in terms of facilities to passengers in stations. Tickets are sold, and passengers provided with information on train running in a station.

The construction of stations are a large part of the cost of constructing a new rail line. This is especially so for underground stations, which need expensive ventilation systems to provide air to passengers, as well as providing an exit clear of smoke in the event of a fire emergency. Stations can, depending on the type of rail system, have a large number of facilities provided to customers, and the large number of these can make construction of the station rather expensive.

Some of the customer facilities that can be provided on a station include:
- Toilets
- Covered waiting areas
- Air-conditioning
- Vending machines and food stalls
- Information of all sorts, including tourist information
- Television screens showing news and other information
- First aid
- Internet kiosks
- Wifi
- Free water
- Mobile phone reception
- Prayer rooms
- Breast feeding rooms
- Lockers
- Services with baggage (such as long term storage)
- Sale of rail related souvenirs
- Shops selling all sorts of products
- Banking facilities
- Library facilities for long journeys

In any one station it is unlikely that all of these facilities would be installed at the same location.

Styles and Configurations of Stations

Stations come in a large array of different configurations, and can be described in terms of a number of simple parameters, which are commonly understood throughout the rail industry. Some of these are:

- Platform length. Typically platforms are raised and higher than both the ground and the track running alongside it, and the length of the platform is same as the length of the train that can sit alongside it, and passengers can board and disembark safely. Not all platforms however are the same length as the trains that stop there.
- Height of the platform. This measurement is taken from the top of the running surface of the rail to the place where passengers stand to board a train.
- Number of platforms. Each platform normally has a separate track alongside it, although in some cases a very long platform may be classified as two separate platforms.
- Number of passengers through the station each day. This is counted through the ticketing system, and the number of barrier/gate entries and exits is counted per day.
- The role the station plays in the operation of the network. Stations may be very large and play an important role in the network or small and trains may stop there only rarely. Some stations are used only for special events. Alternatively, a station can be a terminus, where services terminate and do not continue, or am interchangestation, where passengers can alight from one service on one rail line, and then board a service on another line.
- If the station is underground, at the same grade as the ground, or elevated. These differences are important for the design and use of the station.

Some stations may have disused platforms, and these are not normally counted as part of the total number of platforms. Old stations may have a substantial number of these, and the numbering or identification of platforms may reflect this. At Rockdale station in Sydney platform numbering runs from 2 to 5, as platform 1 is no longer used, and the numbers have not changed since that platform was built over 50 years ago.

The station below is typical of stations in remote areas, and there is only one track at this platform. Trains moving in both directions stop at the same platform. There is no track on the other side. Also note that the station has no roofing, although there is a small area provided, a bit like a shed, where passengers can stand to get out of the rain. Stations of this kind are rarely manned with staff, as there is no booking office for staff to sell tickets at, or store cleaning implements, or any of the other accessories of an office.

A Simple Regional Station

This station has only one track, which has some advantages and disadvantages. A carpark on the side of the station without a track may be accessed without crossing any tracks, which for disabled passengers is a real benefit. Alternatively, the number of trains that can pass through this station will be limited to a small number per hour, as trains moving in both directions will need to pass over the same track. Another configuration possible with thinly used stations is that there ia a loop around the station, allowing trains top stop at both platforms to pass one another.

We can see the facilities provided on this station, which is in outer Sydney. There is no booking office, so no staff will ordinarily be present to help passengers and sell tickets. Seating and lighting is provided, as well as a covered waiting area. The covered area will provide some protection from rain, but given its small size will provide shelter for only maybe 20 passengers, and no more. There are no vending machines, nor any screens providing information on when the next train is due. There are no barriers to restrict entry to the station, and passengers can move around freely. The reader may notice a small yellow box under the orange sign attached to the waiting area, which is a help point for any passengers who feel their safety is threatened. There are no lifts or escalators of any kind.

Whilst this particular station is in a remote area of Sydney, this configuration of station is very common in Australia. There are hundreds of this type of basic yet functional station across the country, and these exist in all states of Australia. They are cheap to construct, and maintain, and perform an important function whilst being relatively immune to damage from vandalism and weather. Some may feel that this type of station is somehow inadequate, but it is an efficient design that performs its function well.

The picture below is of a regional station outside of Paris. We may observe that this station has a clock, covered waiting areas, and is very long indeed. The platform height is also quite low, consistent with the platform heights across Europe and France especially. On the right hand side is a booking office, where tickets are sold, station staff work, and there is an air-conditioned office. Notice that the station has roofing over part of its length. Also notice that the two platforms are on the side of the track, and this configuration is called a side platform station. There is no obvious numbering on the station. Given that there is a waiting area and booking office on one side of the station, and not the other, this station is likely to be a commuter station, which passengers waiting to go to the city centre on one side, and using the other platform to only alight when returning from the nearby city (in this case Paris). This configuration is very common.

A Regional Station in Paris, Side Platforms

The station below is in urban Sydney, and is an island platform station. For this type of station the platforms are in the centre of the tracks, and trains move around the platforms. Passengers wait in the middle of the platform, and can wait in the same place for trains in either direction. Notice on this station there is a vending machine for Coke Cola drinks next to the wall of the old building in the middle of the platform. Express services bypass this station, and local all stopping services, which are slower, stop here with a low frequency.

A Suburban Station in Sydney, Island Platform

Island platforms are often considered superior to side platform stations. This is because:

- Rail staff can be placed in the middle of the island platform, to provide customer information, assistance, and sell tickets
- Toilets, if provided, need only to be located in the middle of the island platform
- In underground systems, island platforms are generally bigger, so there is more room for passengers to wait. For above ground stations stations with side platforms can be any size based on the nearby available land
- It obvious where passengers should wait, but with side platforms passengers need to make a decision.

There are also some disadvantages to island platforms, and some of these are:

- Island platforms are typically larger, and this can particularly be a problem with elevated railways where space is quite limited
- Island platforms require tracks to move in a curve around the station. Notice in the pictures above that the tracks for the side platforms are very straight, whereas one of the tracks for the island platform needs to curve around the platform. If there are high speed trains not stopping at the station this could be a real problem.
- Side platforms can be convenient for passengers with disabilities, as they can enter one platform directly from the carpark. This can be very handy as there is no need to use a lift, assuming that the platform is on the side for trains going in the desired direction
- Island platforms are more expensive than smaller side platforms, especially in underground stations

Another type of station is one where passengers need to request the train to stop, to either board or alight. For heavy rail these stations are relatively uncommon, but for light rail are extremely common. For tram systems this is normal, and the waiting passenger would signal the driver to stop, usually with a movement of a hand. In the US this kind of station is called a halt. There are also a small number of stations like this in Sydney.0020

Stations for tram systems tend to be very simple, likewise for classical "light rail" systems. Tram stations are mostly called stops, and are more like bus stops than stations. Many of the stops are so small that that are almost invisible, and are can only be detected by a small street sign indicating that trams stop there. In some cases passengers may even need to board and alight from the side of the road to the waiting tram.

The photo below is a tram stop in Zurich. It is very basic, and there is an oval building alongside the tram tracks, which has a small number of shops in it. Note that the tram stop is just a flat space with no cover, no obvious lighting, and very little by way of facilities. This is common for tram stops, even in very busy cities.

A Tram Stop in Zurich

The photo below is a light rail station in Hong Kong. Light rail vehicles use this station to move passengers from the main metro line to apartment buildings in outer Hong Kong. From this photo we note that the platforms are quite high from the passenger walking surface to the top of the rail. Older light rail systems had this design, but this is now uncommon. Also note that the entire station is covered, but very poorly lit, and the platforms are very short. The photo was taken when standing on the tracks, something that is allowed with light rail and trams, but not with heavy rail. This station is a blend of a heavy rail station and a tram stop.

A Light Rail Station

In some cases the length of the platform may be shorter than trains which use the platform. Whilst this situation may seem a little silly, in some railways it is common, and passengers can only disembark from parts of the train there is a matching platform next to the door. Where there is no platform next to the train, people wanting to disembark may decide to leap from the train onto the ground below.

Regional trains can be very long because passengers need to sit down, making the passenger density rather low. In some cases platforms where the train stops are not long enough, so doors will face nothing but grass or open space. Furthermore the drop down from the train door may be quite large, and so any passengers that attempt to alight down to the ground are risking injury. In rare cases most of the train may have no matching platform, and disembarkation may be impossible from several carriages of the train.

For obvious reasons it is far better if all platforms are as long as the train itself. In a metro or any other system that operates in an urban environment, this will generally be the case. In some rail systems that operate to remote places, where the number of passengers per day can be counted in the dozens, building a full station may not be appropriate. Alternatively, and this sometimes happens where the station is located next to a river or other body of water, it may not be possible to build a station to the length needed as space is severely constrained, and so a compromise is made. In many cases the local residents may be prepared to accept a reduced length platform as long as there is some sort of rail service.

For any railway that creates this situation there are a number of factors that need to be considered:

- Where passengers jump from the train and are injured, how will medical assistance be provided?
- Can the doors on the train be closed if there is no matching platform? This will require specialised controls to open and close specific doors
- What happens where a passenger does not know that their carriage does not have a matching platform, and cannot alight, and so are overcarried to the next station. Will a taxi be provided? Overnight accommodation? What happens if children are overcarried, is the railway going to allow them to find their own way home if they are overcarried at night?
- Which doors on the train are to be opened? Will it be the front doors or the back ones? Someone in the middle perhaps?
- How can passengers be informed that trains cannot provide exit to certain stations? Perhaps posters on station walls, or announcements to passengers.

Overall if at all possible stations should be constructed to at least the same length as the longest train, but in a small number of cases it may not be appropriate to do this.

Straight and Curved Platforms

Many station platforms in large metro systems are straight, and when trains arrive they will sit in a straight line from one end of the train to another. Many platforms are curved, and not straight, and this is common in large commuter rail systems. In Australia many stations are curved, some dramatically so, as building straight stations was not considered to be important until relatively recently.

A curved platform is shown below. This station is in Hong Kong, and has side platforms. Notice that the platform on the left is concave, and on the other side of the two rail tracks, convex.

A Curved Platform in Hong Kong

The problem with curved platforms is demonstrated in the diagram below. Train carriages are built straight in all cases, and can only bend or articulate where there is a coupling between carriages. Light rail vehicles can be articulated, which means that there can be a number of joins, which allows the vehicle to appear to be curved, but in reality is made up of many short straight sections. Commuter and regional trains especially can have very long carriages, 26 to 30 metres in length is common, and passenger doors will often be located at each end of the carriage. Placing a straight object alongside a curved one will mean that in some places the carriage will be close to the platform edge, and in others far away. In extreme cases the door/carriage floor may be over 30 cm away from the platform, and with such a large gap passengers can fall into it. This may cause injuries, or even death.

The diagram below shows the problem. The centre of the carriage is close to the platform edge, and any doors located there will not have a large gap. Doors close to the end of the carriage, and they are commonly located there on double decker carriages (bi-level), will be further away from the platform.

Figure 5.1 Platform Gaps

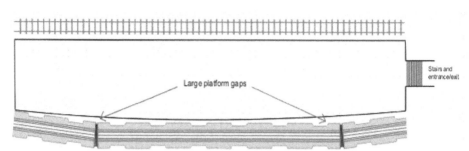

This situation is considered extremely undesirable. Passenger with disabilities, for example those with vision impairment, will struggle to contend with such a large gap, and may fall through. Passengers with wheel chairs will need some sort of mechanical assistance to cover such a large gap, and will not be able to cross this without help. Where gaps of this size exist, stations will need to be manned, and staff provided to allow wheel chair passengers to board the train. Typically a ramp is provided to wheelchair passengers to allow them to cross this gap.

Consider that where this assistance is not provided, and many regional and commuter trains are not staffed throughout the entire day, then wheelchair passengers may not be able to board a train at all. Alternatively, wheelchair passengers may not be able to alight, and may be overcarried to the next station that is staffed or where the platform and the floor of the train are close enough that the passenger can alight without assistance.

Also consider that mothers with prams may also struggle to get onto and off trains. There are a large number of different passengers who are disadvantaged by this station design.

Having said all this, there are some situations where a curved platform is unavoidable. Metro stations and stations will high volumes of passengers should always be designed so that they are straight, and this is a common requirement in the standards for passenger design. However, some very small stations may only have a very small number of passengers, and it may be acceptable for a rail line and corresponding platform to be curved. Consider that there may be laws and regulations that prohibit this in many countries, as this station cannot be used by those with disabilities, even when the number of passengers using the station is very small. This is the case in Australia, and in all future construction all platforms are straight.

Note that curved platforms can be both convex and concave. In diagram 17.14 the platform shown is concave, and this is more common, as island platforms often contain a station building or other facilities in the middle, making the centre of the station wider than the ends. Concave platforms are much more common than convex, as many island platforms have two concave platforms.

So the reader has seen the need to have straight platforms, and the benefits this brings. Building rail lines with straight platforms raises many challenges also, and these include:

- Straight stations are a lot easier to achieve geometrically with side platforms rather than island platforms. Side platforms are not as suited for large passenger flows as island platforms.
- Island platforms, combined with straight platforms, will mean that the rail tunnels leading into a station may need to be twin bore, rather than single bore. A single bore tunnel may be impossible as it would be too large, so two tunnels are needed rather than one. This substantially adds to the construction cost
- Curves along any rail system with straight platforms will need to be sharper, as no curves are permitted along platforms, and curves in most rail systems are very common. In some cases the curves may need to be so sharp that maximum speeds need to be reduced, and so average travel speeds are reduced.
- In severe cases, especially where rail lines are following some geographical feature such as a river or a harbour, it may be impossible to construct entire stations, as the geometry does not permit the construction of a station without curves.

Straight platforms can be difficult to implement, and can present major design challenges. Clever design, and well thought out transport plans, can go a long way to manage this problem.

Terminal Stations

Large terminal stations are places where regional, high speed and commuter trains converge and sit to allow passengers to change from one train to another. This type of central city station is quite common, and in the US and Canada these stations are often called "Union" station. There are union stations in Chicago, Los Angeles, Toronto, and Montreal, and many others. The most famous terminal station in the world is Grand Central Station in

New York. In large cities there might be many terminal stations, for example, in Paris there are six. In all Australian cities there is only one in each city.

Below is an example of a small terminal station. This one is in Perth. Services leave here for some regional destinations, and almost all commuter trains pass through this station. The high ceiling provides a feeling of space. Notice the platforms are numbered, and there are text passenger information displays for each platform. As is common with terminal station, trains are waiting for their scheduled departure times at the station.

Perth Main Station

Terminal stations often have flashy designs to make them look more impressive. Open areas to give a feeling of space and to make the station look sexy and more cool. Large open areas are common in large stations, although there is no real reason why all stations should not be designed in this way.

Interchange Stations

Interchange stations are places where multiple rail lines are connected through the rail station, and passengers must alight to get to other rail lines. Passengers are able to move from one line to another and board another train. Whilst many interchanges are designed well, many are not, problems with transport interchanges can be significant. Some of the more common problems with interchange stations are:

- Two or more rail lines are far apart, and their interchange stations are far apart, and passengers need to walk large distance to get from one to another
- Poor signage means that it is not clear what direction to go to get to the other rail line
- Numerous flights of stair connect different rail lines together, which is a challenge for many passengers to negotiate
- Interchange stations that on maps appear close together but in reality are far apart
- Problems with ticketing, where tickets may not work from one line to another, or passengers need to go out of the paid area to reach the other rail line and do not realise they need to do so
- Some interchange stations are extremely large, and can be difficult to get around due to their size (such as Shinjuku station in Tokyo)
- Walkways between rail lines are little more than construction sites, with poor footing, broken surfaces, barriers around construction work, and poor signage.
- In some cases there may be multiple stations to interchange with, and signage needs to identify which is the correct one for passengers to walk to, and to get to their final destination.

The ideal construction of interchange stations should allow passengers to easily and quickly move from one rail line to another. Ideally, interchange stations should have platforms close together, so that the interchange time is small. Good station design will allow passengers to interchange without going to far, and in Hong Kong it is possible to interchange between rail lines by moving from one side of an island platform to another. This is done by designing stations so that trains arrive on two sides of a platform moving in the same direction.

The photo below shows a moving walk. A moving walk is similar to an escalator, but along flat ground. Moving walks do not have stairs, and are there to assist passengers in getting quickly from one place to another. Moving walks are common in airports, and also in large interchange stations. There are a number of large moving walks installed in stations in Hong Kong at interchange stations. The moving walk shown below is located at the Domestic Airport station in Sydney, where it is used to connect the two terminals together though the underground station.

A Moving Walk

Components of a Station

Platform screen doors have become increasing common around the world. They are suited in metro stations or at stations where there is significant crowding. To work properly the doors on the station need to line up with the doors on the train, and this is usually only possible with ATO (automatic train operation), where a computer drives the train. A human driver will rarely be accurate enough to allow a rail system to use platform screen doors.

Overall platform screen doors seem to be becoming more common, especially in Asia. Below is a picture of some platform screen doors in Singapore, and as with just about everything in Singapore, it's very clean and shiny. The platform screen doors below are full height, and completely the station from the tunnel in which the train moves.

Platform Screen Doors

Platform screen doors have a number of benefits, including:
- It is very difficult for people to commit suicide at stations with platform screen doors
- No one will be pushed under a train from overcrowding with platform screen doors
- The air-conditioning load for the station will be lower, as the air from the station will not mix with outside air
- The station looks better, as passengers cannot see the dirty tracks and tunnel, but instead see the clean shiny platform screen doors.

No discussion of any asset in a rail system would be complete without mentioning the disadvantages:
- They are expensive
- They can fail, and this can delay trains
- Their use is limited to trains that are at least partially compute controlled, as drivers cannot stop their trains with the accuracy needed to position the train next to the platform doors.

The lines painted on the floor to direct passengers. These are common in major metro lines where the number of passengers is very large. Passengers alighting move through the middle of the doors, and on the outsides wait for passengers to alight before boarding the train.

The doors above are full height doors, but it is not necessary to do that. Below is a picture of some platform edge barriers in Tokyo, which provides many of the benefits of full length doors. In terms of passenger flow and safety the half height doors work quite well, but do not assist with air conditioning. Also note the advertising screens on the walls across from the platform.

Platform Edge Barriers

Concourses are the area above or near a station where many of the entrances and exists are connected. Passengers move throughout a station from the concourse, and it is often above the station. The photo below is of a metro station in Hong Kong. Long concourses like this are common in underground metro stations, where the station has the additional purpose of allowing people to move around the city without catching a train. In the front of the picture are the barriers that provide entry into the station proper, and on the left is a walkway to the other end of the station. The concourse here is above the platforms where the metro stations stop, and as the metro trains are quite long, the concourse also is quite long. The area behind the barriers is sometimes referred to as the "paid area", where passengers need to buy a ticket to enter.

A Metro Station Concourse

Some of the stations in Hong Kong serve as major thoroughfares without the need for passengers to catch a train. Pedestrian interconnections through a railway station can be beneficial to the movement of people around the station. Stations may be connected through overpasses, and passengers can walk along these to get to the next station without riding a train. In some cases pedestrian overpasses or shopping centres can extend for several kilometres, connecting several stations together.

The picture below is of a station in Osaka where the platforms are on both sides of the train, and doors are opened simultaneously on both sides of the train. In practice passengers enter form one side and exit from the other. This type of station is sometimes called the Spanish solution, because it is commonly used in the Barcelona metro. Passengers get on through one side of the train, and alight from the other. This structure of station is able to move more people quickly.

Barcelona Style Platforms for a Terminus Station in Osaka

The station configuration above is sometimes used in terminus stations, and in stations with very high numbers of passengers. This configuration can be very effective in reducing dwell times.

Passenger information is a very important in a rail system. Information provided to passengers can be much more than when the next train arrives although this is also very important. The picture below shows a simple rail passenger information screen in a metro station in Paris. The information is very basic, but provides what passengers need.

Passenger Information Sign in Paris

Information about the local area can also be provided to passengers. This includes exits, where important landmarks are located, and how to get there from where passengers are standing. This is called wayfinding.

Maps should be provided and easy to read. Network maps in particular should be freely installed in any station. Below in the two smaller photos are geographical maps provided in two different stations. The one on the left is of the metro network in Tokyo. The one on the right is the regional rail system of Taiwan.

Geographically Correct Maps in Stations

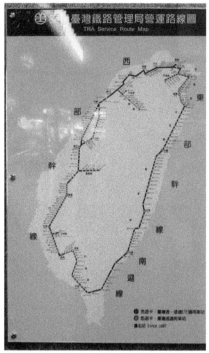

Tickets are sold on almost all rail systems, and provide a right to passengers to ride on the system. Paper tickets, previously very common, are a type of ticketing system called "proof of payment", where customers buy a ticket and use that ticket as proof of purchase. Tickets are almost always sold on stations.

Becoming more common are smart cards, where money is added to the card and then it is used to gain entry to the station. Smart cards obviate the need for large numbers of paper tickets, and more commonly money is added to smart cards through credit cards and machines specifically provided to do this. Providing enough ticket machines is very important. Below are some ticket machines in Western Australia. On the right is an add value machine, which is used to add money on to their smart card. In the middle are the machines for selling old style paper tickets.

Ticketing Machines in Perth

Stations are places where large numbers of people move through each day. Advertising can be a very valuable source of revenue, and many railways take advantage of this and build different types of signage and information. Stations can be a very good place to locate advertising signage, and all sorts of different products can be promoted through signage. In Hong Kong signage is very common, and much of the flat space is devoted to signage.

Advertising is not limited to signage. This display is for digital cameras, in a display cabinet in Thailand. This one is at Chit Lom station in Bangkok, and seems to contain actual digital cameras. Promotions in stations for different products can take a variety of different forms.

The photo below is of a different type of passenger information. Very long trains, in particular regional and HSR trains, have numbered carriages and can be very long. Their length, and use of reserved seating on HSR trains, means that passengers need to know where their carriage is located. For HSR services where the dwell time is only a couple of minutes at any one station, passengers need to know where their carriage is located along the platform, and so these signs are provided along the platform to provide this information.

Passenger Carriage Information

Bins can be provided on stations, but with the increase in terrorism, many of the bins were removed from stations in Australia. The fear was that terrorists would place a bomb in the bin, then leave, allowing the bomb to go off and them to escape. A solution was found to this problem by having transparent bins. In theory any bomb would be seen before it would explode. The picture below shows this type of bin. The photo was taken at Tokyo high speed station.

Transparent Rubbish Bins in Tokyo

Underground and elevated stations in major rail systems are almost always protected from the rain. There is complete coverage of the railway station, and heavy rain will not effect the movement of passengers and trains. In regional or commuter systems, almost all stations will be above ground, but not elevated, and be exposed to the elements. The station below is common in some rail systems and the covered area is very small. This station is in Perth in Australia, and like many stations in that city has almost no coverage of the platform.

An Uncovered Station

For small stations there is no real reason why the entire platform should be covered. During rainstorms passengers can wait under the small shelter provided, and this will be adequate in most cases. For larger stations, lack of coverage can be a problem, as passengers will want to avoid getting wet, and will all wait under whatever cover is provided. Where the covered area is small, it will be come very crowded, and when boarding any trains there will be delays are the passengers will all crowd into one or two doors. This can create serious problems with dwell time, as passengers will attempt to board trains only through train doors next to covered areas.

Stations that are only partly covered will need less cleaning, as rainwater will wash away any dirt, especially where the station is designed with a slight slope on the platforms to allow rainwater to run away. Sunlight can sterilize the floor of any platform, in time, so this means that sanitising agents may not be needed to clean the platform. As a general rule, stations should only be covered if needed, and there is nothing wrong with leaving a station partly uncovered.

Access in and out of Stations

Trains are large, and in many cases there are two or more tracks making up any rail line. Passengers need to be able to get from outside the rail corridor to the desired platform to catch a train. They need to either go over the top of the rail corridor, or beneath it.

The raised section over a station is called the concourse. Concourses are quite common, and often stairs may lead to the concourse from both outside the station, and from platforms.

The design below is a common one, and the concourse is connected to both the platform and the outside of the station through a ramp, and not stairs. For a side platform, where there are no barriers, this solution is quite acceptable, and there are only two ramps at this station, one in view and the other to the left. The ramp allows passengers to get over the tracks entering the rail corridor. Also the ramp allows wheelchair passengers access across tracks.

A Station Ramp

Ramps are a cheap and practical solution to providing access to stations for those with disabilities. Ramps also are unlikely to fail, and require very little maintenance, unlike lifts and escalators.

There are national and international on ramp design. Normally ramps must be design to be below a certain grade, and a steep ramp will be difficult to those with disabilities to use. Also, long ramps need to have landings, which is a flat space where people with wheelchairs can rest during the ascent of a ramp.

An alternative to a pedestrian crossing over a station is for passengers to cross at the same grade as trains. The pedestrian crossing above is a common way to allow passengers to cross the rail tracks, but obviously there is a safety risk. The trend in modern railways is to avoid using this type of infrastructure, as there can be fatalities to the travelling public.

A Station Lift

Mobility aids are a very important topic with stations. Adding mechanical aids to a station will help disabled people use the station more effectively, but they can be very expensive to install. On the left is a lift which can move people from the concourse to the platform. This type of free standing structure is extremely expensive to install as there is no other structure upon which the liftwell can use for support, and so it needs to be a free standing structure.

Escalators are often also used to move people from and to the platform. Escalators are very popular because the speed up the departure of people from the platform once passengers have alighted. Escalators can be provided individually, in pairs, or in groups of three or more.

A Station Escalator

A final word on stations; they are really a very key part of any rail system. Stations as what passengers first see when they enter the rail system. The key to designing good stations sees to be:

- Easy and safe movement of passengers onto and off trains
- Passengers can enter and exit the station quickly
- Good facilities for people with disabilities
- Convenient help points and other stations facilities
- Maximisation of revenue from advertising and shops
- Cost effective design.

Light Rail Stations

One of the advantages of light rail and tram systems is that they can be designed with little separation between the rail system and road vehicles and often at the same grade. This reduces the cost of construction, and makes them very accessible to public transport users, as they are at street level and usually not buried deep underground. In many cases these systems have no separate right of way. Trams often operate down the middle of roads, and in many ways are treated the same as any other road vehicle.

As light rail and trams are located in and around roads, the question arises as to the placement of track and rail corridors in comparison to where roads are located. The right of way for rail may or may not be separate from road vehicles, and a large number of different configurations are possible, and some of these are shown below:

The figure below shows a rail corridor in the middle of a street, with road vehicles on either side. This is a common design for light rail stations, and the use of a separate right of way for rail track is a good idea. For this design passengers will need to cross the road on one side or the other of the station to exit the corridor. Passengers will also need to cross the tracks to get to the other light rail station to go in the opposite direction to the one in which they came.

Figure 5.2 Light Rail Station in the Middle of the Street

Below is another configuration for a light rail station, and the light rail station is on the left. The road is separate from the light rail station, although alongside one another. The light rail station is an island platform, so passengers will need to cross one track to get to the side of the road. This configuration is a very good one, as road and rail traffic is separated.

Figure 5.3 Light Rail Station on the Side of the Street

The light rail configuration below is extremely common in tram systems, but is also used in light rail systems as well. Road vehicles and rail share the same right of way, and mix freely. Whilst road vehicles can overtake trams, the converse is not true. This structure can work quite well, and is common in Melbourne with the large tram network there. One of the drawbacks with this structure is that passengers who wish to board and alight onto the tram must cross roads with fast moving vehicles on it, and the potential for an accident is quite significant. This configuration, whilst cheap and easy to implement, is not the safest, and is generally not recommended unless it cannot be avoided. There are however, many instances in a large tram network where there is no alternative, and this configuration is suitable.

Figure 5.4 Mixed Light Rail and Road Traffic with some Separation

Also notice with the above configuration that road vehicles drive on the steel rails that support the light rail vehicle. Where the width of the road vehicle and rails are the same, it is possible for the road vehicle to slide along the rails, and not be able to stop when needed. This is particularly a problem in the wet, and accidents can be quite common.

The light rail configuration below is a poor one, but also somewhat common, especially in Melbourne. There is no separate right of way for rail traffic, and so road vehicles and trams/light rail share the same space. There is no way for road vehicles to pass the rail traffic, which is likely to be slow. As trams/light rail stop to allow passengers to board and alight, these vehicles will stop and wait at the tram stop. As the rail vehicle waits at the stop, road vehicles need to wait also. For a very busy street, passing through a congested shopping area, the travel speed of the tram/light rail vehicle may be very slow, to the point where there is no point in providing the service at all.

Figure 5.5 Mixed Light Rail and Road Traffic

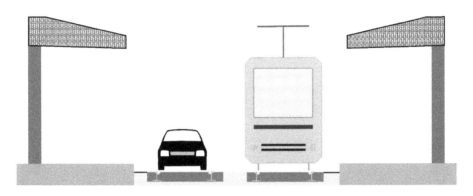

Tram systems were once very common in many parts of the world, especially Europe and North America. Almost all of them have been removed, and only a small number exist in their old form. One of the major contributing reasons for this was the use of the configuration above, which blocked road traffic and greatly contributed to congestion. The survival of the Melbourne tram network, now the world's largest, was because the configuration used above was rarely used, and so problems with congestion were avoided. The configuration above should only be used when absolutely necessary, and when there is no alternative.

Chapter 6 Other Infrastructure

A rail system comprises different elements that, put together, make a working system. The obvious main elements have already been discussed, but there are some others that are not quite as obvious. Trains, stations, and infrastructure, are all key components of any rail system, but there are other parts of a rail system that are important, but probably not as well known. This chapter focuses of these lesser know aspects of rail systems.

Passenger information systems

Passengers need information on when trains are arriving and on which platform. Passenger information systems (PIS) provide this information to passengers, and this can be provided through a variety of different media, such as display boards, telephones, announcements, or through the internet. Recently many railways have set up systems so that apps on smart phones can be installed so that real time information can be obtained for trains and their movements.

Below is a picture of passenger information screens in Central station in Brisbane. This system provides information on when trains are arriving and leaving, and what platform they are on. This system is a good one, and passenger information is clear.

Passenger Information Display

Information other than train running can also be provided to passengers. For example, where train lines are removed for service for major maintenance or upgrading, then information can be provided to passengers on when and where this is happening. Alternatively, when trains are delayed, information should be provided to passengers so that they know where to go to get buses, or what the forecast is for the resumption of services.

The photo below shows an old style timetable display. The older style was able to present a lot of information, and this one has a clock above and the stopping pattern below. In red are the interchange stations. At this station there are two platforms. The name of each station is painted onto a block of wood, which can be turned to display the relevant information for the next train. Whilst this system looks primitive, and it is, in practice it worked quite well. Clearly the station needs to be manned so that staff could come out and change what is displayed after the passage of each train. This type of system has become uncommon, and computerisation has resulted in the removal of many of the timetable displays like the one below.

Wooden Timetable Passenger Display

Stabling

In almost all rail systems trains do not operate constantly all day. When not in revenue service trains need to be stored somewhere, and the area where they are stored is called stabling, the same word as where horses are kept. Trains are said to be "stabled" in the yard. When stabled trains are often turned off, or have the power removed from them, and the air conditioning switched off to save power.

When trains are stabled train crew need to exit the vehicle, and remove power. Usually staff depots will be located next to the yard where trains are stabled, so staff can go the toilet, get changed, and eat meals. Stabling yards are very important facilities, and much of the management of a railway occurs in and around where trains are stabled.

The picture below shows some stabling in Cronulla in Sydney. The yard is empty because all the trains that are normally stabled there have departed and are in revenue service. Notice the long walkways, and lighting, which is common for stabling yards.

Commuter Train Stabling in Sydney

Some limited maintenance may be performed on trains. Some stabling yards contain more than just stabling, and some maintenance may be performed. Where a lot of maintenance is performed, the yard may no longer be described as a stabling yard but as a maintenance centre. This type of facility plays a large role in the operation of any rail system.

The placement of stabling yards can be an important question for railways. For metros and commuter systems stabling is usually located in a place where land is cheap, and far away from the centre of the city, and preferably, in a place where the noise of moving trains around won't disturb anyone. Light rail stabling may be located closer to the centre of cities as journey distances can be shorter.

For commuter and regional rail systems, the placement of stabling yards is much more important. As many commuter trains start in remote areas early in the morning, and then travel to the city, they often end their journey close to or at the centre of a city. In the afternoon the same trains need to return back to their origin, taking the same people back to their homes at night. This means that two stabling yards are needed, one at the far end of the rail system, and another in the centre of the city, where land is very expensive. Having a stabling yard in the city can cause significant problems, land is scarce, and a stabling yard is not a pretty thing, and valuable land is wasted. Alternatively, to send the trains out to the origin, which may be 2 or 3 hours away, means additional travel time on the train, which costs money, and additional wages for the crew to take the train back to the origin. Once there the train will need to return to collect the passengers who want to get home at night. So a regional and commuter service will need to stable trains close or in the centre of the city.

One way of managing this situation is to build the stabling yard, and then build over the top so that the land is still used effectively, and the stabling yard is not visible. Another is to build the stabling underground, which is expensive, but again eliminates the problem.

Maintenance Centres

Maintenance centres are places where rollingstock is maintained. Rollingstock, like any other equipment, needs maintenance, and it needs to be performed somewhere. Maintenance centres can be very large places, as heavy equipment is needed to perform the maintenance. Staff numbers at maintenance centres may also be large.

Maintenance centres may perform some of the functions of a stabling yard, and yes trains can be stored there. However the main purpose of a maintenance centre is to provide the maintenance train needs, rather than overnight storage.

Train maintenance, like maintenance on aircraft, is performed at certain intervals. Small maintenance tasks, such as inspections and minor adjustments, are performed at frequent intervals. The more major the maintenance is, the less frequently it is performed. Some maintenance will be performed, monthly, some yearly, and some less frequently than that. Largest of all maintenance is usually when the entire train is stripped down, and many of the major components replaced or refurbished. This is very expensive, and should be done only when needed.

The larger and smaller maintenance need not be done at the same place. For example, the refurbishment of trains can be done in one centre, and the smaller maintenance tasks done in another. Alternatively, the washing and cleaning of trains may be done in one place, and the routine inspections and minor maintenance done in another. Many combinations are possible.

There seems to have been a trend in modern railways to get the manufacturer of rollingstock to maintain it as well. Often this arrangement is created when the rollingstock is ordered, and the manufacturer will need to build a maintenance centre. This adds significant cost to the purchase of rollingstock, but can be a good way to manage maintenance. This system is commonly implemented in Australia. Bombardier maintains a significant part of the rollingstock in Melbourne, for example.

Control Centres

A control centre is a place many of the functions associated with a train system is controlled. One rail system may have a number of different control centres. A control centre is typically composed of a small number of people, with some screens relaying information relevant to the rail system, and some phones. Some of the functions performed by a rail control centre can be:

- Controlling the movement of trains, contact with drivers, and making decisions about where trains should go during unforseen events and delays
- Control of the electric power grid that supplies power to trains. The power system for any railway is surprisingly large, and needs someone to monitor and control it
- Monitoring the safety and security of passengers, usually through CCTV and help points. CCTV stands for closed circuit television and rail staff can see what is happening to passengers, and if anyone needs help. Staff monitoring the security of passengers will often have a close relationship with the local police force
- Incident response for engineering failures, such as the signalling, communications or track system. Qualified staff can be dispatched to the site of any failure, and remedy any engineering fault.
- Monitoring the safety of tunnels, such as the ventilation within tunnels and fire safety. Many modern tunnels have complex fire and safety systems, which require someone to intervene in the event of an emergency. This function is important, but often there is little to do but monitor the tunnel with trains passing through it.

- Passenger information such as train running information and delays if any to train services. Information can be provided to passengers for a variety of different scenarios.

All of the functions listed above will be consolidated into a single control centre, but there is no reason why this should be so. In some cases, in a very large network, the network may be split into smaller parts, and a consolidated control centre will manage all the functions for that smaller area. In other cases, the functions listed above might be separated into many different control centres, and a very large railway may have dozens of control centres. Separate control centres can exist for each large tunnel. Managing the flow of communication between each of these control centres can be an interesting challenge.

Control centres may or may not include the functions of a signal box. For the most part signal boxes are separate establishments, and operate independently of any control centre.

Signal Boxes

Signal boxes are an important part of most rail systems. Trains travel throughout the rail system, and when approaching junctions a decision is needed on where the train goes. In most cases the driver within the train is prevented of setting the direction the train goes. Drivers are able to set the speed, and start the train moving or stop it, but usually cannot change points to set the train in a different direction. In some tram networks the driver can set the route, and in a small number of freight networks this can also be done, but mostly train drivers cannot set points and send a train in a different direction. Drivers can also set the route in a small number of junctions in Melbourne, from within the tram.

The picture below shows a tiny signal box that controls a level crossing in Sydney. There are still many signal boxes that protect and control road level crossings, and there is a signaller in the signal box waiting to lower the level crossing so that a train may pass. It might seem a little quaint to manually control a level crossing, but it is still done in some places in Australia.

A Small Signal Box

The points and their direction are set by the signalling staff in a signal box or control centre, and these can be located almost anywhere. The people working in signal boxes can see the position of different trains, and as trains pass through junctions, and where points are set. They set the points so that trains can move through the junction. Signalling staff perform a job that is sometimes seen as being a bit boring, and there has been a trend to create software to perform the same function. Where this is done, fewer rail staff may be required to manage the movement of trains.

Signal boxes are something that is usually common in a regional or commuter network. Metros have very few junctions, and so don't have as many signal boxes. Some rail systems, such as a national system such as in Switzerland, have a very large number of signal boxes, and in 2011 SBB had 538 signal boxes in operation. That's a very large number, and a correspondingly large numbers of people would be employed in working in signal boxes in this rail system.

Mush of the work associated with running a railway is performed in a signal box. It's the place where trains are actually managed, and sent on different paths. In aviation, the equivalent is air traffic control, which performs the function of directing planes into airports and through controlled airspace. Signal boxes also serve as places where information is collected and disseminated on what is going on in the rail system, and drivers call signal boxes to inquire as to what is going on when equipment fails, or they are delayed, or there are problems on the network, or to report any incident. A signal box is a key piece of infrastructure, and its importance cannot be understated.

Behind signal boxes are the control centres. In some cases a control centre may assume the functions of signal boxes, and this is common in newer modern rail systems. In large rail systems, the split between signal boxes and control centres seem to have continued.

REFERENCES

1. Infrabel, *Network Statement*, Version of 9/12/2011

2. banedanmark, *Network Statement*, 2012, Jan 2011

3. Liang, H. & Ning, Z. & Yana, S *Analysis and Selection on Fare System of Urban Rail Transit*, Advanced Management Science (ICAMs), 2010

Chapter 7 Freight Infrastructure

Introduction

Freight is an important part of any economy of any country, and the efficient fast and cost effective movement of goods is critical to productivity and maintaining low prices for goods, and hence international competitiveness. Rail freight went through something of a decline in the 60's and 70's, and despite reports of the death of the rail freight industry, it is still alive and well, albeit a bit smaller in percentage terms compared to road transport.

Freight systems have some different infrastructure to passenger networks. Obvious differences are the terminals, where goods are loaded and unloaded. Less obvious are the weighbridges, where freight trains are weighed, so that the freight operator can be billed for the passage of freight trains through a network. Other infrastructure includes marshalling yards, refuelling depots, and more unknown infrastructure such as hot box detectors to inspect bearings in the axles of freight wagons. Rail freight requires a lot of specialised infrastructure.

One advantage rail freight has is its fuel efficiency. Road vehicles such as trucks and articulated vehicles require more fuel than rail, so for intensely used freight corridors, rail freight can still be viable. For mines with large amount of material to be moved, rail freight works quite well, and so large rail lines often service mines. The energy efficieny gives rail a niche market for freight movements, and this justifies the installation of freight infrastructure.

Overview of Freight Systems

Almost anything can be moved by rail freight, and almost any item that is sold or manufactured can be moved by rail. For example, washing machines could be moved by rail, or milk, or books, almost anything. What can be moved by road or air can be moved by rail. The choice of transport mode is an important one for any freight system, and this decision can have a large impact upon costs, delivery times, and punctuality.

To provide the reader with an idea of the broad range of goods that can be moved, consider the list of different goods below. It is not at all an exclusive list, but provides some indication of the broad range of goods that an be moved by rail:

- Whitegoods and furniture
- Food products
- Livestock
- Animal products, such as wool
- Bulk food products such as wheat or milk powder
- Petroleum products
- Gases of all types such as chlorine
- Liquids used in production process such as ethanol or methanol
- Bitumen or other organic compounds
- Lumber
- Minerals and bulk materials such as coal, iron ore or sand
- Parcels
- Weapons, such as tanks or missiles
- Road vehicles, cars and trucks
- Mail
- Industrial machinery
- Sugarcane

Many different products can be moved by rail. In competition with rail, the main transport modes are:
- Road freight, which means mostly trucks. Road freight is more flexible than rail, and often suited to short distances or small numbers of shipments
- Air freight, which is used for long distance freight, and where the item is needed to be transported quickly. Air freight is very expensive and struggles to compete with other transport modes
- By ship, which are mostly ocean going. This transport mode is frequently the only serious way to transport goods from one country to another that is not linked by land.
- By barge, a type of boat that is suitable for large navigable rivers. Barge transport depends on the location of suitable rivers, and whilst not common in Australia is still common in the US.
- Other more unusual means of transporting products, including dedicated pipelines, or conveyors.

Freight trains are quite different to passenger trains, although some of the design concepts are the same. Some of the key differences are:
- Freight trains accelerate and brake much more slowly than passenger trains

- Freight trains are almost always much longer than passenger trains, and are often over 1 km long
- Freight trains can be diesel or electric, in Australia freight is mostly diesel
- Freight trains have difficulty climbing grades, and even small grades can be a problem
- Passenger trains often have powered passenger cars (EMUs), freight trains are almost always powered by separate locomotives
- Passenger trains are rarely divided and amalgamated, freight trains are often split and recombined
- Freight trains are mostly much noisier than passenger trains
- Freight trains are almost always much heavier than passenger trains, and frequently do much more damage to the infrastructure than passenger trains
- Freight trains are limited to an economic speed of about 100 kms/hr, although there are exceptions to this rule. Passenger trains often are much quicker than freight trains.

Australia has a number of very successful freight rail systems, which are able to survive and thrive because of the high price of coal (which at the time of publishing this book has changed substantially), and the energy efficiency of moving bulk materials by rail. Successful rail freight companies, which in Australia can even generate enough revenue to pay for the infrastructure and signalling, move very large quantities of coal for export to overseas markets, mainly China and Japan (in that order). The volumes of material moved are truly extraordinary, and by weight rail is by far the most commonly used mode of transport for freight in Australia.

The photo below shows a typical freight locomotive. Large and extremely powerful, these locomotives can be combined together to be able to generate the motive force to move large number of wagons. The fuel consumption of diesel locomotives can be very large, although it should be noted that freight trains can be very fuel efficient compared to the loads they are moving.

A Freight Locomotive

Maintainers of rail infrastructure tend to dislike rail freight, and this is because of the changes in infrastructure needed to accommodate freight trains. Broadly, more infrastructure is required, and some of the infrastructure required is different to what is normally required for passenger services. Some of the changes/additions to rail infrastructure include:

- The spacing between signals is increased, so the headway increases, even for passenger trains. This can be extremely inconvenient when a small headway is needed
- The track structure needs to be stronger to accept freight loads that are normally much heavier than passenger loads
- Freight trains have paths through the rail system that are different from passenger trains, and normally more junctions will be needed to accommodate those paths. For example, passenger trains, especially commuter train, operate from the city to the outskirts of large cities, but freight services may move from one remote part of the city, to another remote part, in a direction completely different from the passenger traffic. These different direction may require substantial amounts of additional infrastructure (turnouts commonly)
- Some sort of billing system is needed for the freight trains, as access to the network is often based on the number of wagons and the weight of the train. Whilst in theory it might seem ok to trust the freight company when they provide data on what trains went where, experience in Australia has shown that freight companies will understate the loads on their trains. Weighbridges are needed to weight trains are they enter the rail network to accurately bill freight companies for the trip through the rail system
- Freight companies will need marshalling yards, where wagons are combined into trains, and where locomotives are stored awaiting use. Marshalling yards can be very large, and are not pretty to look at, and so any rail network with large amounts of freight will need to have at least, and maybe several of different sizes

- Freight trains are often not as reliable as passenger trains. This is frequently because passenger trains use electric power, and operate as EMUs, and so have natural advantage compared to freight trains. This means that they break down more frequently, and there needs to be a system of "recovery" or "rescue" of broken down trains. A normal high powered locomotive is often enough to rescue a broken down freight train, but there are also speciality rail vehicles that perform a similar function. Rescue is often provided at a fee, and a failed freight locomotive will block the rail line in at least one direction, depending on where it has broken down. This needs to be considered in the design of any freight system

- Freight trains pull wagons that can have a bearing failure, which can derail the freight train. Special infra-red cameras are available to look for heat in a rail wagon, and this system is often called a "hot box" detector. These will be needed in strategic places around the network to prevent large derailments

- Facilities will be needed to store freight trains when faster moving passenger trains need to pass. Alternatively, the freight train may need to wait to get access to a freight terminal, because it is full, or there is a curfew that prevents the freight train from entering a certain area of the network at a certain time. Freight trains seem to spend a lot of time waiting, and sidings, or sometimes called a refuge. Will be needed at strategic places in the network. Passing loops can also be used.

- Special precautions may be needed before hills to ensure that freight trains do not stop before a hill. Whilst freight trains will be able to start moving on level ground, and climb moderately steep grades, if they stop on a high grade they may not be able to pull the load up the grade. Special signals may be needed to ensure that once a freight train enters a section of track before a steep grade, that there is nothing to stop the train on the grade, until the track is in a place where the grade is lower. A freight train may need 10 kilometres of clear track to ascend a particularly steep grade, and stopping halfway through the climb can mean that the freight trains gets "stuck". In Australia this special type of signal is called a "tonnage signal", which will tell the driver of a freight train that the road (ie the rail track) is clear and that it is ok to proceed at normal speed for several kilometres.

- Freight trains are often diesel hauled locomotives, and these produce diesel fumes. Whilst this is fine in the open air, in a tunnel the fumes can rapidly build up and create a toxic environment. In a narrow tunnel the diesel fumes will need to be removed, and this means additional ventilation. A rail tunnel with mixed freight and passenger traffic will need very good ventilation systems to ensure that the air is acceptable to the passengers, and not smell or be full of soot. Ventilation systems in tunnels are expensive

- Modern intermodal container freight trains are often "double stacked", where a second set of containers is placed on top of the first. Where this is done the height of any overhead wiring will above the containers will need to be extremely high, maybe as high as 7.5 metres, and this can impose a substantial cost to have either the overhead wiring moved higher, or built high when first installed.

The damage caused to a rail system from freight can be quite significant, especially where the rail freight is very heavy. The main damage to the rail system is the rail and supporting infrastructure, which will be "pounded" by the heavier loads. Damage to the infrastructure consists of :

- The top of the rail will develop metal defects, such as flat spots and cracks
- Trains carrying bulk loads will often drop some of their load onto the rail track, fouling the ballast and filling points/turnouts with coal or grain or whatever material is being carried. This can cause many problems, especially with the points filling with this unwanted material, and this if often a problem at the entrance to the final terminal where the bulk material is unloaded.
- The track infrastructure will degrade with the constant passage of heavy trains, and need more frequent maintenance

Many types of passenger rail systems cannot accept freight onto their system. If anything freight on a rail system is becoming less common for a variety of reasons discussed below. Some of the rail systems that cannot accept freight, or rarely do, are:

- Metro systems, where the high frequency of service makes it almost impossible to fit freight trains in between passenger services
- Light rail, where the track structure is rarely strong enough to take large freight trains, and freight trains are rarely suited for running down the middle of streets (although freight trams still exist and were common in Australia for decades)
- Monorails, which are utterly unsuited for freight trains, unless the monorail has been specifically designed to accept freight
- High speed rail, where the slow speed of freight trains will not permit HSR trains to operate at their normal commercial speed. HSR freight

is something that does exist, and is discussed extensively in Chapter 16, but is quite rare.
- Some specialised rail systems, especially medium capacity metros that operate with rubber tyres, are not suited for freight

Some of the passenger rail systems that are better suited to accepting freight are:
- Commuter systems, where the heavy commuter trains run on infrastructure that is often the same as what is required for freight
- Long distance and overnight trains, which are often not high speed, and so can intermingle with freight trains quite effectively.

Some of the different types of freight are:
- Bulk materials, such as coal, iron ore, grain, milk, fuel, sand, flour, gypsum, etc
- Intermodal freight which consists of large metal containers. Intermodal freight is very important, because this is how most items are shipped around the world today
- Other more unusual freight types, such as steel coils, or road vehicles. In theory many different types of large materials may be moved, should a freight wagon be designed to move it.

The photo below shows some of the different types of freight wagons that can be used. At the front are flat cars, in the middle hoppers for powder of different types, and then after that tank wagons for transporting liquids.

A Freight Yard

There are a number of useful numerical terms that can applied to a freight system. These can be used to describe many aspects of a rail freight system, and some of the key parameters are:

- Axle load. This measure normally has the units of tonnes, and there are mostly 4 axles per freight wagon, so the axle load is the weight of the wagon divided by 4. Freight companies often want to operate with the highest possible axle load, as this increases their efficiency, and reduces the number of trains needed. A typical limit for the axle load would be about 20 tonnes, depending on the freight network of course. In Australia some railways have been able to achieve up to 40 tonnes per axle.
- MGT, which stands for Million Gross Tonnes, which is one measure of the number of tonnes that have been moved through the network in any given year. The measure is made at one point, and the same network will normally have different MGT figures throughout the network. A network with a low number of freight trains may only have an MGT of about 5, and with a moderate amount may have 10 to 15 MGT, Some freight systems in Australia have only 100 MGT, or even over 200, which is a very large amount
- GTK, which stands for Gross Tonne Kilometres. The GTK represents the weight and the distance that freight has been moved, and it is the multiplication of the number of kilometres travelled, by the distance the train has travelled. GTK numbers are often very large, and so are commonly quoted in millions of GTK. A rail network with only a small number of trains may still be able to have a large GTK figure if their trains travel large distances.

A freight corridor is a dedicated rail freight line that does not have any passenger traffic. Freight corridors can move large quantities of freight, and are very popular with freight operators. The safety risk of freight is much lower than for passenger trains, a freight train can have a derailment where many of the wagons are derailed and destroyed, and there is no loss of life because the freight locomotives are the only places where there are any people. Freight corridors are a very effective infrastructure strategy, and can be spectacularly successful in increasing rail freight movements. Many of the problems associated with moving freight are eliminated, the higher priority given to passenger trains, the lack of network capacity, and curfews that are often placed on freight movements are all eliminated as types of problems.

One problem that commonly arises in freight networks is balancing loads between destinations. It is common for intermodal trains to operate between only 2 destinations, and pick and deliver at both ends. What is desirable is for the loads and freight traffic to be balanced, and so the same number of intermodal containers, or really any other freight traffic, to be the same in both directions. This will reduce cost as the cost of the train is spread over a larger number of containers. In practice things are rarely so nice, and often there is a much higher flow of freight in one direction than in another, and so in one direction trains operate at capacity an in the other are only partly full.

Bulk materials freight almost always has fully loaded wagons and trains moving in one direction, and empty ones in the other. In Australia trains make their way from mines to ports, so that raw materials can be exported, and there is nothing to bring back from the port to the mine. As a result bulk material trains almost always operate half the time full, and the other half empty. This is very difficult to avoid.

A derailment is when train wheels no longer sit on top of the rails, and in severe cases can lose contact with the rail entirely. Derailments are one of the major safety risks for any railway, and for passenger trains this risk should be kept to an absolute minimum. For freight systems derailments have a much lower risk, as the locomotive will rarely derail, but wagons can and often do, especially towards the back of the train. Derailments are much more common for freight trains than for passenger trains. Many freight systems have dozens of derailments per year, and this is because the risk associated with the derailment is so much lower, so mitigations to prevent derailments are not as commonly applied as for passenger trains. Given the relative frequency of derailments, any significant freight system needs to have a method or re-railing any derailed freight train. There are a number of methods for doing this, and a common and easy one is to use jacks to lift freight trains up and back onto tracks.

Freight trains are almost always driver by a human driver. Many freight drivers consider the driving of a freight train to be an art, and requires a special skill. Recall that freight drivers mainly control the speed and braking of a train, and mostly cannot control direction. Managing the acceleration of a freight train is apparently quite difficult, and mistakes can result in separated trains, damage to rail, slow movements of freight, and safety risks. In Australia there have been attempts to automate the driving of freight trains, especially in large mines in the desert where salaries are very high, and up until the writing of this book these attempts have been almost entirely unsuccessful. This may change in the future, as research is continuing into this topic.

Rail Freight Lines

Rail freight lines have some differences from rail passenger lines. The structure and loading gauges need to be larger than a minimum size, and the track infrastructure needs to be quite strong. Many rail lines do not permit the movement of any freight over them, as they are not designed to allow the movement of freight trains. A rail line that allows the passage of freight will need to be designed to allow freight to pass over it, and including freight is a conscious decision that a rail planner will need to make.

Once a decision is made to allow freight through a rail line, then there are some design considerations that need to be taken into account. The grades that a rail system passes over is very important to a freight operation/train. Freight trains are very heavy, and climbing a hill requires a lot of power. The more steep the grade, the more power that is required. A large grade, such as 3% can be climbed by a freight train, but this requires more locomotives, which are expensive, and so freight companies prefer to use as few locomotives as possible. Where there is only one high grade along a rail corridor, the freight company will need to put more locomotives onto a freight train to get over this one hill, something that is inefficient to do.

It should be remembered that passenger trains can climb high grades. Some light rail vehicles can climb grades of almost 10%, which is extremely high. A rack and pinion railway can allow for grades even higher than this, and 12 or 14% is possible. The grades for a rail freight system are far lower than this, and a freight train would need to be specially designed to allow for a grade of even 3 to 4%.

The largest grade on any freight path is called the "ruling grade". It has this name because the highest grade will determine how many locomotives are needed, and this is an important parameter for any freight movement. Freight train movements will be more profitable when the ruling grade is low, and so only a small number of locomotives are needed. In Australia the ruling grade is often high, because there is a mountain chain running from the top of Australia to the bottom, along the eastern seaboard, and there are many rail lines that have comparatively steep grades because of this.

Where the ruling gradient is very high, or comparatively high for a freight system, there is greater load on the wagons closer to the locomotive than at the end of the train. Rail wagons are all connected together in a long string, and the force to pull the end wagon is passed through the wagon second from the end, and so on. In some cases the weight of the wagons is such that the stress and load on the wagons near the locomotives is so great that there is a risk that these wagons will be damaged. Care may need to be taken in position the right wagons close to the locomotives, which can accept the higher loads. Other strategies for managing the forces on freight wagons is to put multiple locomotives in different positions in the freight trains, so that the load on any one wagon is not excessive.

Passenger rail lines are mostly duplicated, which means that there are two tracks so that trains moving in different directions are free to pass one another. Rail freight lines are often only single track, especially in Australia, where track maintenance costs are high and the number of freight movements is low. Single line tracks allow the movement of trains in both directions, and a track that has this feature is said to be bi-directional. Freight lines that are single track need a place for trains moving in different directions to pass one another.

A passing loop is a section of track, along a single line section, where the track is duplicated. Where tracks are uni-directional a passing loop may be on one line, to allow trains to pass. Many freight lines have very low volumes of traffic, and need only one track. Freight trains moving along this rail line, in opposite directions, will need to pass each other, and the purpose of a passing loop is to allow this to happen. One train will be held in the passing loop, waiting for the other, and then when the other reaches the passing loop then the first train is free to proceed.

A Passing Loop

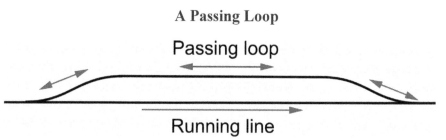

Passing loops are common, especially in areas of single track. Single tracks are much cheaper to maintain, and are very common in Australia. To get more capacity out of a single track line, passing loops are necessary. For a freight system with low amounts of traffic, many rail transport projects may include the construction of passing loops.

Passing loops are also needed where passenger trains and freight trains share the same track for long distances. As freight trains are limited to about 110 kms/hr, passenger trains that move faster than this will be unable to pass the slower freight train. One solution to this problem is to build a passing loop, allowing freight trains to sit in them whilst the passenger train passes. To achieve this the passing loop needs to be long enough to allow the freight train to sit in it without intruding onto the mainline. The lengthening of a passing loop is a good way to cheaply improve the capacity of a rail freight system.

Structure and loading gauge are very important for freight trains. Narrow and low structure gauges will result in small freight wagons that are not economical, and cannot carry the goods or the containers that are needed. Small loading gauges will result in the use of small freight wagons to fit into the space allowed, and so to transport the same amount of material more wagons are required, which will be more expensive, and sometimes not possible because of restrictions on the maximum length of freight trains. Structure and loading gauge also arise as issues when double stacking for intermodal containers is needed. Double stacking requires a much higher loading gauge, which if often not available.

Different Types of Freight

Bulk Material Freight

Bulk materials includes bauxite, coal, iron ore, sand, wheat, etc. In Australia the three largest bulk materials moved by rail freight are coal, iron ore, and grain. Bulk materials are particularly easy to load and unload into wagons as they can be poured, rather than lifted with a crane or individually handled into the train or onto a wagon.

Below is a photo of a coal train passing through suburban Sydney. This particular train is empty, and notice that it is quite long and the end of the train cannot be seen. Also note that it is passing a suburban rail station, and there are occasionally injuries to passengers who attempt to "touch" the passing freight train.

Coal Freight Wagons

The coal, or similar bulk material, can be poured, using gravity as the motive force. Not all bulk freight moved is solid, some is liquid. The freight wagon in the photo below was used for moving milk, although based on its condition has not been moved or used for a while. Sometimes the freight wagon below is called a tank wagon. This one is quite old, at least 30 years, and has seen a lot of use.

Liquid Wagon for Freight

Bulk material freight is often more economic and profitable than intermodal freight. The relative wealth of companies who move bulk materials means that they operate their rail operations differently; their trains are often in much better condition than intermodal locomotives, they can brake more quickly and have a superior braking curve, and can pay higher prices for paths through complex networks.

Intermodal Freight

After World War II increasing trade volumes placed great pressure on ports and transport systems, and there was a need to develop a better way of moving goods from one place to another. In the 1950 a trucking company owner called Malcolm McLean developed the modern shipping container, which was a standard size and can be used to move a large variety of different goods. The key advantage of the shipping container was its standard size, which meant that trucks, rail wagons, and ships could be specially adapted to move the containers.

Shipping containers, also called intermodal containers, can be moved on almost any transport mode. The containers are strong, durable, and can survive bad weather and rain. They are easy to move and transport, and can be placed on top of one another. Each corner of the intermodal container has a locking mechanism called a "twistlock", that allows containers to be secured to each other when they sit on top of each other. The twistlock mechanism also allows the container to be placed onto transport, such as ships, trains, and trucks, and then locked into place so that it does not fall off when the vehicle bounces around of passes through heavy seas. The introduction of the intermodal container has been one of the great successes of the 20th century, and has revolutionised the movement of freight worldwide.

Intermodal containers come in many different types. Whilst the early versions were little more than steel boxes, modern intermodal containers can be quite different to one another. Intermodal containers can be refrigerated, for the shipment of ice cream, and other foods that need to be frozen. Containers can also have air conditioning, or ventilation. Bulk containers are also available, suitable for moving bulk materials much like the specialised wagons in the section above. Also available are container to move dangerous goods, which have special flooring to contain spills, may be have special insulation, and of course have different signage.

Intermodal freight is a very important part of any modern economy. Whilst in Australia intermodal freight is often seen as the poor cousin of bulk material freight, in many countries and especially the US, intermodal freight is a very central part of the transport system. The US has a high rail intermodal freight share, with rail moving 35-40% of all intermodal containers countrywide.

Intermodal containers come in many different sizes, but are classified according to their volume. The standard intermodal container is 20 feet long, and 8 feet wide and 8 feet high. In metric units this corresponds to a length of about 6 metres, and a width and height of about 2.44 metres. Intermodal containers are wider than rail gauges, and so will overhang the rail gauge. Recall from chapter 8 that trams are typically 2.45 metres wide, and light rail 2.65, and metros about 3 metres (9.8 feet), so intermodal containers are about the same width as a tram. High shipping containers are also available, and these are about 2.9 metres in height.

Intermodal containers seem to be limited to carrying about 28-30 metric tonnes of goods, regardless of their length or height. Containers often weigh about 3 to 4 tonnes, so the gross weight of a container should not exceed 32 tonnes. For most rail systems that is not a lot of weight, and most railways should be easily able to accommodate this amount of weight on one wagon. Where double staking is employed, even 64 metric tonnes is easily carried by the right rail wagon, and with 4 axles on the rail wagon this corresponds to a per axle load of about 16 tonnes, not a large amount for most heavy rail systems.

It is a commonly held view that moving intermodal containers by rail is only economically viable when the transport distances are very large. By large this can mean over 500 (around 310 miles) kilometres, or even further, over 800 kms. This is quite a large distance, and many countries and not this wide or long, especially in Europe where many countries are very small. In the US, Australia and Canada this is not a particularly large distance, and freight movements of this distance are common. In Europe a 1000km (620 miles) freight movement would almost definitely require transport through 2 or more countries, or in some cases more than 5.

Below is a photo of an intermodal container loaded onto a train. This particular one is quite unremarkable, and seems to be relatively old. Notice that the container is a nice square shape, and it's quite long, so probably 40 feet in length.

An Intermodal Wagon

One each corner of the container is a device called a "twistlock". It is on the corner that containers are secured to each other, and onto other objects. To secure a container effectively requires a matching unit underneath the container, and if needed, on top.

Intermodal containers are rated according to units of Twenty foot Equivalent Units (TEUs). The standard intermodal container is 20 feet long, so a 40 foot long intermodal container would represent 2 TEU's. Most containers now moved worldwide seem to be the 40 foot or longer container, rather than the shorter containers.

The table below shows the TEU rating of different sizes of containers.

Container size and TEU rating	
8 feet high x 8 feet side by 20 feet long	1 TEU
8 feet high x 8 feet side by 40 feet long	2 TEU or 2.25
8 feet high x 9 foot 6 inches side by 20 feet long	1 TEU
8 feet high x 8 feet side by 48 feet long	2.4 TEU

8 feet high x 8 feet side by 54 feet long	2.65 TEU

The TEU is a very important unit of measure for intermodal shipping. Trains and terminals are rated in terms of the number of TEUs moved. A typical intermodal terminal might move 100,000 containers per year. This does not mean that 100,000 containers were moved, only that the total TEU ratings of all the containers add up to that figure

Intermodal containers are often stacked on top of a rail wagon called a flat car. Flat cars, as the name would suggest, are entirely flat, and can be an excellent way of transporting many types of goods, in addition to intermodal containers. The photo below shows a modified flat car that is used for moving intermodal containers.

A Flat Car

The photo below shows a well car, where the container sits lower to the track, and is contained within the sides of the wagon. This type of wagon is useful because the container is held more securely, but also because the height of the top of the container can be a little lower, which can be useful where the structure gauge of the freight line is restrictive. Well cars are particularly useful where the track gauge is wider than standard gauge, ie, broad gauge.

A Well Car

In Australia rail is more competitive than road for moving bulk materials even over short distances, and the economic distance where road transport is more competitive than rail is very short indeed, perhaps 20 kilometres or even less.

For bulk materials where the amount moved is relatively small, the freight task may be performed with a road transport to a rail hub/terminal, and then moved by rail to its final destination.

Double stacking is a method of transporting more intermodal containers for a given train length. A second layer of containers is stacked on top of the first layer, and so more containers can be moved than a single stack. Double stacking is very common in the US, where it is widely considered to have dramatically improved productivity. In the US it is common for governments and private companies to have considered investing in their local rail systems to allow double stacking, and many of these reports have been published to the internet.

One of the main advantages of double stacking is the reduction in cost. As more containers can be moved, and the weight of containers is normally not that high, for a given locomotive it is often possible to move more containers. This increase in volume moved per locomotive results in a cost decrease, which for the highly competitive freight market is very important.

Overall the effect of double stacking is to either reduce train lengths or to increase the capacity of trains. It is not the case that introducing double stacking can reduce the length of trains by 50%, in practice there is a reduction of maybe 25-30% in train length, as not all intermodal containers can fit together or sit on top of one another. Some of the more heavy containers cannot sit on top of lightweight or weak containers, as it cannot be guaranteed that the lower container won't be damaged. The table below shows which configurations are acceptable and which are not.

Often the sidings where freight trains are loaded with containers is not the ideal length, and too short. Double stacking allows an increase in capacity for a train of a given length, and this can be very important where sidings are too short. In remote areas land will often be very abundant, and so rail sidings can be almost any length, but around ports the length of sidings may be very restricted. Allowing double stacking is one way of making more efficient use of scarce land around ports, as a train of a given length can move more containers when double stacked.

Double stacking requires higher structure and loading gauges than single stacked trains, and this is the major reason why double stacking is so difficult to achieve in practice. Typically the height/structure gauge required is about 6.5 metres (21 feet), although a loading gauge of 5.9 metres(19.3 feet) will also allow two standard height containers to be placed one on top of the other. Even a loading gauge of 5.9 metres is quite a lot, and the loading gauges of many rail networks is about 4 to 4.5 metres. Increase the loading gauge is not cheap, and an increase of 2 metres (6.5 feet) is a large amount.

Some of the changes that are needed to achieve double stacking include:
- Increasing the height of tunnels. This can be done either by boring out the top of the tunnel, or reducing the height of the floor of the tunnel, or both.
- Increasing the height of any overhead wiring that is used to supply trains with traction power, or removing the overhead entirely
- Raising bridges, and many bridges on a track designed only for single stacking will be very low to the track and the train, and raising bridges is a standard infrastructure investment. Raising bridges is not cheap, and depending on the local roads, can be extremely difficult to achieve in practice

Intermodal terminals need to redesigned and changed to accommodate double stacking, where intermodal trains are double stacked.

Other types of Freight

It is possible to move many other types of freight, other than bulk materials and intermodal containers. Rail wagons can be customised to move almost any type of freight, and in Australia the main type of freight that is moved is steel products and coils. The steel coil is manufactured in a large steel mill and then shipped for final processing or for export. The photo below shows steel soils waiting to be shipped Australia, in a custom designed rail wagon.

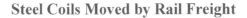

Steel Coils Moved by Rail Freight

Piggyback operation is a type of freight system where semi-trailers (lorries) which are carrying freight are themselves put onto the train, and then transported. The driver of the truck or semi-trailer will get out of the vehicle and then sit in a special rail car where many drivers can sit. This type of system is rail in the Chunnel, the rail tunnel that runs from the UK to France.

Freight Terminals

The design of terminals is very important to any rail freight operation. Passengers get off trains by themselves, however rail freight does not unload by itself, and needs to be removed. Bulk freight is often easier to unload, and intermodal freight is lifted off the train using a crane, or a forklift truck specialised designed to lift containers. Terminal design can be influential in determining what freight transport mode is common in a country or area. Well designed terminals can greatly assist with reducing the cost and time required for successful freight operations.

Any terminal needs to be designed for the type of freight that moves through it. An intermodal freight terminal is not suitable for use as a bulk material terminal, and vice versa, so there might need to be several terminals catering for different types of freight in one area or region.

Modern intermodal terminals can perform some of the functions of international border clearance, such as customs and quarantine. It is more efficient, and better for the senders of the containers, for these government checks to be performed at the same place as where the container is dropped off and delivered to. Intermodal terminals might also offer ancillary services, such as cleaning of containers, or repairing them if they are damaged. Some containers may need to be disinfected, and this service can also be offered for a fee. Perhaps the most important service is to store intermodal containers, as they are not expensive to buy, and companies often buy too many, or have procured some for freight movements that only occur occasionally. The storage of shipping containers does not generate much revenue, but it is an important function in support of intermodal freight.

Freight terminal are often linked to ports, where goods can be exported and imported. In rare cases goods may be taken to a port to ship to another port in the same country, although for reasons that are not clear this is unusual in Australia. Small countries will normally have only a small number of ports, and would not ship containers from one port located close to one another.

Bulk material freight terminals are often located outside large cities, in a regional area. Material shipment such as coal or grain, destined for export, does not need to pass through a major city, and doing so only adds cost and time. On the other hand intermodal traffic is often destined for major cities, much of the contents of intermodal containers are consumer goods, and these end their journey in a shop or retailer.

Freight terminals that move intermodal containers can be classified on the basis of the number of containers moved through the terminal per year. Some references discussing intermodal freight traffic distinguish between terminals that move more than 10,000 TEU's per year, and those lower than that being a small terminal. Some major intermodal terminals handle millions of TEU's per year, and a terminal that handles less than 10 thousand is really quite small.

The photo below is of the intermodal terminal in Yennora in Sydney. The train sits in between the two long gantries, and the gantry crane moves along the length of the train to remove or place intermodal containers onto the train. This type of lifting arrangement is more efficient than a diesel powered container forklift, but more expensive to construct.

A Intermodal Freight Terminal and Gantry Crane

Below is a photo of the coal bulk terminal no 1 in Newcastle. This terminal is structured as a giant loop, and freight trains arrive, move around the loop, and unload their coal onto a conveyor, which moves the coal to where it is stored. Many of the coal freight terminals in Australia have some limited storage capacity, called a stockpile, where coal can be stored for a short time until loaded unto a ship for transport to the final consumers. This particular coal terminal loads ships with coal, and they are not in this photograph. The large orange machines are coal loaders.

A Coal Freight Terminal

Many terminals have restrictions placed upon them by government as to their hours of operation. Many terminals in Australia are required to close at certain hours. The placement of a terminal, especially if it is placed in an industrial area that has no housing, will give the terminal a better chance of being permitted to operate longer hours.

Freight terminals are often built on a slight grade, allowing wagons that are de-coupled to move slowly in one direction. In the past it was common for freight wagons to be uncoupled, and then be allowed to move slowly downhill under their own weight, but more recently this practice is banned in many places and all freight movements and marshalling of wagons to be performed with locomotives. In Australia all movements of wagons in yards are now done by locomotives. Not withstanding that, it is convenient for a freight yard to be on a slope, as this makes runaways much more unlikely, and if they do occur, in a consistent direction.

Different Configurations of Freight Terminals

There are many different possible designs of freight terminals. The freight terminal needs a structure that supports the operation of the freight that is moving in and out. Some freight trains are all unit trains, where the train is not divided, and moves only one product, and it is moved directly from the terminal to destination without storage or stopping. A unit train operates on a loop, and moves slowly around the loop when it is being both loaded and unloaded. The terminal design that is shown below is called a balloon loop, and these are often attached to mine. The train enters the balloon loop, and then moves around the loop, being filled with whatever bulk material is being shipped. Whilst it is possible to combine a balloon loop with intermodal freight, this combination does not seem to exist in Australia.

Figure 7.1 A Balloon Loop

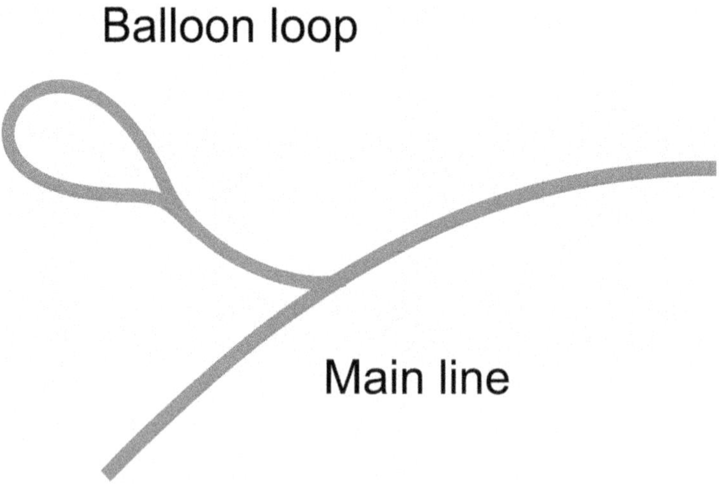

Balloon loop

Main line

The great advantage of a balloon loop is that the train moving through it does not need to be divided and/or shunted, it can slowly move around the loop and receive its cargo. This type of configuration is more efficient than a pure siding. Trains that use a balloon loop may not need to have wagons added or removed, and will travel empty to the balloon loop, and then full when taking the bulk materials from the balloon loop to where they need to go, often a port but not necessarily so.

Below is a freight terminal that is more suited for intermodal freight. This terminal is relatively small, and intermodal terminals can be very much bigger than this. This terminal allows trains to enter, and then one or other of the freight roads would allow loading and unloading. As the terminal is structured as a passing loop, locomotives can be moved from one end of the train to the other.

Figure 7.2 A Simple Freight Terminal

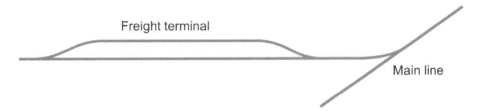

The schematic below shows a more complex freight terminal, one where it is possible to store a number of trains at the same time. Often in this type of freight yard it is possible to drive a road vehicle around the entire yard, as the rails may be buried quite deep into the ground, so that it is easy for road vehicles to climb over the rails. This type of terminal can be useful for using a forklift truck to put goods and freight onto the train, especially if the yard is not particularly full most of the time.

Figure 7.3 A Freight Termnal with Storage

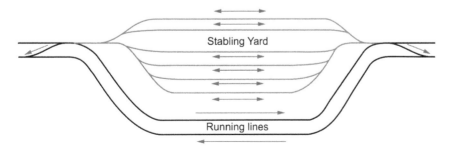

Another common configuration with freight yards is to put a diamond crossover in the middle. The freight yard is essentially split into two halves, with the crossover allowing movement between the two halves. The purpose of the crossover is to allow trains from any one road in the left freight yard to get to any road in the B yard, and vice versa. This type of configuration allows for the efficient storage and management of freight trains.

Figure 7.4 Freight Yard with a Diamond Crossover

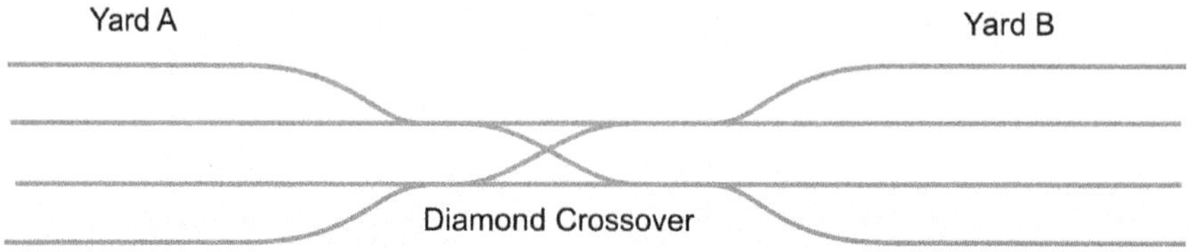

Yard A   Yard B

Diamond Crossover

Chapter 8 Structure/Loading Gauge, Geometry, Heights and Grades

Track is at the centre of any rail system. Most of the infrastructure sits around the track, and the size and position of the track is important to how the infrastructure is laid out. Grades influence that infrastructure around the track, and stations for example are typically placed the grades are low.

Track and space around the track is very important for the choice of what rollingstock can use the track. Many different types of trains cannot accept large grades, and where the space around the track is small then the rollingstock will need to be small as well. In many ways, the track will affect many other rail systems, which is why it is so important. This chapter presented the basic of broadly describing some features and the space around the track.

Loading and structure gauge is a term that applies to the space through which a train moves. Structure gauge is the space that the infrastructure must stay out of for a train to make its way through a rail system. This includes platforms, where platform edges must not intrude into the structure gauge to the point where a train will strike the platform when entering a station. Platform strikes are uncommon, and when they occur can cause serious damage to a train. Usually the paint is stripped from the side of the train next to the platform.

Loading and Structure Gauge

Railways have specific terms for describing the space required for a train to pass through on a network. These terms are commonly used, and understood between countries. These terms are a rare example of some jargon that is used in Australia/UK and the US interchangeably. They are:
- Structure gauge
- Loading gauge
- Kinematic envelope

The structure gauge is a defined space around the track, into which no equipment or infrastructure is permitted. If any equipment strays into that space, then a train may strike it as is comes past. The structure gauge is the space allocated to trains to pass along the track and is larger than the train that passes through it, to allow for movement of the train and any possible slight deviations of the train from its design size. Trains are never as large as the structure gauge.

Structure gauge is what infrastructure maintainers use for maintaining clearances. They need clear cut guidance on what the structure gauge is, and any large railway and many smaller ones will have detailed standards on structure gauge and what sizes are required. It is not sufficient for an infrastructure maintainer to be told the loading gauge, as this is information is not useful and cannot be used for maintenance purposes.

The loading gauge is the area in which a train must fit in when stationary. Loading gauge is relevant to rollingstock and its design. It's important because the loading gauge determines which trains can be procured, what size they are, and hence their capacity. Loading gauges play an important role in determining the capacity of a system.

The kinematic envelope is the space through which a train might move, taking into account superelevation (cant), the suspension of the train, the end throw and centre throw. Calculating the kinematic envelope is a process called dynamic gauging. Calculating the kinematic envelope can be a paper exercise, and there are formulas that describe how to do this. The kinematic envelope increases where there are curves, as the curves result in the end of the train protruding away from the track.

Whilst changes to structure gauge are a common type of rail transport project, the cost can be high. Changes to structure gauge are very expensive, and can involve large scale changes to infrastructure. To complete a change from one structure gauge to a larger one, every point in a rail system or rail line at that structure gauge needs to be converted, it's not sufficient to convert some or even most of the track. There is no benefit for doing most of it, and so one problematic point in a rail system can stop the conversion to a larger structure gauge.

In many cases the maximum possible loading and structure and loading gauge is difficult to change. Train lines often pass next to structures and buildings that cannot be moved or demolished, and so it is not possible to change the width of the train, or the space through which the train passes. Some stations are heritage listed, and so major changes are not possible. In these cases rail operators need to manage their rollingstock as best they can, given the constraints on size. Problems with the maximum permitted size of trains can be very expensive to manage.

Loading gauges do not need to be square or rectangular. The diagram below shows a typical profile of a loading gauge. The shape down below is typical of what a loading gauge outline looks like. Whilst not always this shape, they often are, and so a train that is a perfect rectangle would not be permitted to operate on many rail networks if it were above a certain size.

Figure 8.1 Typical Loading Gauge

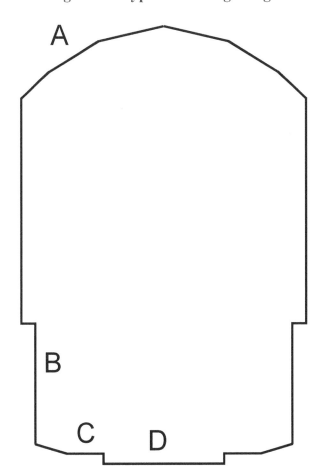

The letters in the diagram above refer to various parts of the outline. These are:

A/ This is the curved part of the roof of the train. Most passenger loading gauges are curved, and this allows the construction of arch shaped tunnels, which are cheaper to construct than tunnels with rectangular ceilings in many cases.

B/ There are often cut-outs for platforms for passenger trains. There is always a risk that passengers will fall between the train and the platform, and it's best if this gap is kept as small as possible. One way of managing this is to have the train overhang the platform, so that the gap is minimised.

C/ For the bottom of the train the loading gauge is flat and even all the way across, and is higher is some parts compared to others. In the schematic above the corner is cutout(same as D). This is to allow the many different types of rail side devices to operate and exist. Also the ballast is sometimes too high, and so contact with the ballast is minimised by having the train higher than the track.

D/ This is the lowest part of the train, and where the train runs along the track.

The kinematic envelope should be within the structure gauge, even for curves. If the kinematic envelope extends to the structure gauge or beyond it, then trains may strike objects and structures next to the track (such as platforms). The kinematic envelope needs to fall within the structure gauge.

One way to determine the kinematic envelope is to run different trains along the track and see what happens. Whilst this is possible, it is far better to calculate the kinematic envelope, because if a train strikes an object it tends to make a bit of a mess, and the damage can be substantial. Also once a rail line is constructed it can be a bit difficult for the structure gauge to be changed, so any errors can have a very long term impact. So for most rail projects, the kinematic envelope will be calculated first before construction begins.

So of the things that need to be considered in the calculation of a kinematic envelope are:
- The superelevation of the track
- Track movement
- The suspension of the train
- Loads on the train, for example, fully loaded passenger trains compared to empty ones
- Rail wear
- Tilting functions of trains, including both passive and active tilt
- Curves in the track

Structure, loading gauge and the kinematic envelope are most relevant to a railway in tunnels, but are also important at stations and particularly at platforms. Tunnels have very limited space available, and increasing the size of the tunnel once constructed is a messy and expensive business. If a train can't fit into a tunnel, there is little a rail organisation can do to get it to fit in, other than making major engineering changes. Some things can be done, and trains with hard suspensions and very little movement in the springs that support the train can move through slightly smaller tunnels. Also, trains that move at lower speeds can also fit into smaller tunnels, as they bounce around less when moving at lower speeds. Where a railway needs to move a large train through a small structure gauge, this can sometimes be achieved with dramatically reducing the speeds of the train to a point where the railway is confident that the train will not strike any object.

If a train strikes an object (again, such as a platform) the result can be very bad indeed. Whilst a glancing blow may not be very serious, a full impact with a fixed object is really a train crash, and passengers can be killed. That's really bad, so railways will put a lot of effort into ensuring that trains cannot collide with anything fixed. One of the key responsibilities of maintenance staff is to ensure that a collision does not occur.

Vegetation often will grow into the space where the train runs. Trees often line rail corridors, and as trees grow they can come into contact with passing trains. This can be very common in some networks, and it's common in Australia. It's mostly harmless for trains to brush alongside trees, and most tree branches are quite soft. Trees can present problems to the overhead wiring system, or reduce the visibility of signals so that drivers cannot see them. In these situations trees can be a problem, or when they fall over in a big storm this can also block running lines.

In some cases trees may be planted on stations. The branches of trees may grow to the point where they intrude into the structure gauge, and even strike a train. Trees on stations, where they are healthy and continue to grow, will need to be routinely pruned to keep them outside of the structure gauge

It has become common to calculate the movement of trains, and the swept volume resulting from this, with software, and some packages have been written which work quite well. The software can visually display and calculate the movement of trains through tunnels, and so any problem areas that need to be addressed are identified. Whilst a hand calculation is possible, this method is increasingly rarely used. The calculation of the structure and loading gauges and a key part of the planning process, but given the technical detail necessary, and the cost, and the level of detail needed to carry out the analysis, this would typically be done very late in the process (but definitely before construction).

Loading gauges, as mentioned above, often have complicated shapes. To simplify things, they are often described in terms of height and width.

Figure 8.2 Simplified Description of Train Size

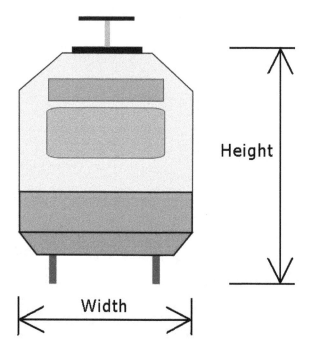

The pantograph above the train is not normally included in the loading gauge. In practice the pantograph is spring loaded so it can move up and down, and can usually be pushed down almost flat with the top of the train. Where the pantograph sits there is usually a hole/recess so that it can be strapped down, i.e. when transporting the train by sea. The space in which the pantograph is sits into is called the pantograph well.

Below are some common loading gauges. It is only a small selection of the large number of loading gauges currently in use. Worldwide there would be hundreds of different loading gauges.

Table of Loading Gauges

Country	Name	Width	Height
UK	W6	2820 (9 feet 4 inches)	3965 (13 feet)
	W7	2778 (9 feet 1 inch)	3966 (13 feet)
	W9	2996 (9 feet 10 inches)	3967 (13 feet)
	C1	2744 (9 feet)	3772 (12 feet 4.5 inches)
(high speed)	UK1	2720 (8 feet 11 inches)	3965 (13 feet)
US, Canada, Mexico	AAR plate B	3250 (10 feet 8 inches)	4620 (15 feet 2 inches)
	AAR plate C	3251 (10 feet 8 inches)	4720 (15 feet 6 inches)
	AAR plate E	3252 (10 feet 8 inches)	4800 (15 feet 9 inches)
	AAR plate F	3253 (10 feet 8 inches)	5180 (17 feet)
European Union	UIC-A	3150 (10 feet 4 inches)	4320 (14 feet 2 inches)
	UIC-B	3151 (10 feet 4 inches)	4321 (14 feet 2 inches)
	UIC-C	3152 (10 feet 4 inches)	4650 (15 feet 3 inches)
Germany	G1	3153 (10 feet 4 inches)	4280 (14 feet 0.5 inches)
	G2	3154 (10 feet 4 inches)	4650 (15 feet 3 inches)
Spain/Portugal	Iberian gauge	3300 (10 feet 10 inches)	4300 (14 feet 1 inch)

Superelevation (Cant)

Superelevation is the difference in level between the two rails. It is common for the two rails to be at different heights, and it is a very useful thing to do in many different situations. The height different between the two rails is show below.

Figure 8.3 Simplified Description of Train Size

Superelevation is also called cant. Superelevation is installed in track to allow trains to be able to move through curves faster, and so reduce travel times. It is a cheap and effective way of improving the efficiency of track.

Platform Heights

Standardising platform heights in a rail network greatly aids efficiency and reduces cost. This is the ideal, and new modern networks are constructed such that all the platforms are the same height. However, in many older rail systems, there is more than one platform height, and potentially there could be several different standard heights.

Platforms are may not be at the same height as the train floor. It is preferable for modern train systems to have the platform as close as possible to the floor of the train, and at the same height, but this often does not happen. The photo below shows the regional tilt train in Taiwan, and note that the floor of the train is higher than the platform, and there is a step between the train and the platform.

Taiwanese Train with Door Flaps

Platform heights installed in rail systems have been decreasing over time. This is especially true for trams and light rail, where platform heights are dropping significantly. Trams often run at street level, and stepping into a high floor tram can be quite daunting, especially for people with disabilities. It's best for disabled people getting into trams to have the floor as low as possible. It is seen as desirable to reduce the height of platforms as much as possible, and rollingstock manufacturers are often keen to announce any reductions in floor heights of their products.

The step fills the space between the train and the platform. The step is often slightly higher than the platform, so that if the platform is curved or too close to the train then the step won't hit the platform.

It is engineering challenging to make the floor of the tram very low. Ultra-low floor trams have had some significant engineering problems, with cracks developing in the body of the trams, which were quite serious and needed substantial repairs. The lower floor puts higher forces on the body of the tram, and these stresses can cause higher maintenance costs and maintenance problems.

Ultra-low floor trams, notwithstanding their engineering problems provide a better service to customers. The step up into the tram is a small one, often only 180mm, which is low. This is enough for people to comfortably enter the tram from road level, and so this technology is still being developed (and perfected).

Low floor trams are higher than ultra-floor trams, and are about 300-350mm from the ground or platform, or about 1 foot in the English imperial system of measurement. Most p can negotiate this kind of step up from the road.

Higher speed trains will generally require higher platforms, at least as high as 550mm. The higher platform allows for structural changes in the rollingstock that make it stronger, and allow for higher speeds. Trams and light rail vehicles with ultra-low floors are limited in speed to about 100 kms/hr, or perhaps even lower.

There are many different platform heights in use around the world today. The variety is enormous, although attempts are being made to standardise to specific heights. It seems that 550mm is the minimum height for larger commuter trains, although 760 mm platforms are also used. In Australia and Hong Kong platform heights of 1100mm are used, which is high enough that if passengers fall off the platform onto the tracks then they will injured from the fall.

Where the platform is a different height to the floor of the train, the preference is to make the floor of the train higher. Passengers will step up into the train, and not down. It is considered by some that it's dangerous for passengers to step down into a train, and so this configuration is avoided if at all possible.

Rarely rollingstock is designed that can accommodate different platform heights. This can be achieved through steps that can vary in height to allow for the different platform heights. Rollingstock with this feature can be very expensive.

European Union decision 2002/735/EC specifies that high speed trains should be designed to a platform height of 550mm or 760mm. However, for trains that operate in the UK 915mm was specified, and for the Netherlands 840mm was specified. Even within a standard designed to force uniformity between member states, there is significant differences in the platform heights.

In designing a new rail line or more stations, and where platform height are different throughout a network and there is a need to extend the system, system designers face a number of choices:

1/ modify the existing platforms to a standard height

2/ have two different sets of platform heights, and different rollingstock that is designed for each

3/ continue with different platform heights, and order specialised rollingstock that can accommodate different platform heights.

4/ Design very long platforms that have two different heights, and so able to accept different trains with different floor heights

It's always best to have one standard height throughout a rail system, but there are many examples where this was not possible.

So overall we can observe the following with platform gaps:

- The higher the platform gap, the higher the structural stiffness of the corresponding train
- Lower platforms provide a better service to customers
- Platforms heights have steadily reduced over time in many countries

Grades

Grades and their presence in a rail system changes many things. Rollingstock needs to have larger motors to climb the grade, or more locomotives. Also maintenance on the rail infrastructure increases for grades. Where the grades are especially large specialised trains are needed to negotiate the grades.

Grades should not be installed at stations where possible. In some cases it may be necessary to install a grade at a station, but this is very undesirable, and should only be done where absolutely necessary.

Grades are calculated as below:

Figure 7.4 Grades

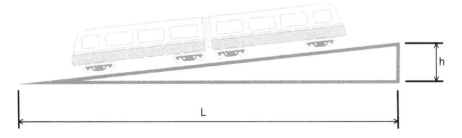

Grades, or sometimes called slopes, can be expressed as percentages, based on this simple formula:

$$Grade = \frac{height}{length} \times 100\%$$

In Australia and the UK grades can be expressed as 1 in X, where X can be found from the formula below:

$$\frac{1}{X} = \frac{height}{length}$$

Which can be re-arranged to give:

$$X = \frac{length}{height}$$

Another way of expressing grades is using this symbol (‰). This symbol is similar to a percentage, but actually means the parts out of 1000. So a 1% grade would be expressed as 10‰. This symbol is common in continental Europe, for the maximum possible grades that a particular type of train can climb. On Wikipedia the symbol is referred to a *"per mille"*, which is Latin for per one thousand.

So, the conversion tables for the grades are:

Grades and Conversions			
%	**UK/Australia**	**Degrees**	**‰**
1	1 in 100	0.57°	10
2	1 in 50	1.15°	20
3	1 in 33	1.72°	30
4	1 in 25	2.29°	40
5	1 in 20	2.86°	50
6	1 in 16.6	3.43°	60
7	1 in 14.3	4.00°	70
8	1 in 12.5	4.57°	80
9	1 in 11.1	5.14°	90

Grades and Conversions

%	UK/Australia	Degrees	‰
10	1 in 10	5.71°	100
11	1 in 9.1	6.28°	110
12	1 in 8.3	6.84°	120
13	1 in 7.7	7.41°	130

Most rollingstock is quite limited in the grade that it can climb. Common limits for the grades that rollingstock can climb are listed below, with some comments:

Maximum Acceptable Grades

Rollingstock type	Max grade	Comments
Trams	6% or 10% with specially designed rollingstock	Some trams are specially designed to climb high grades
Light rail	6% or 10% with specially designed rollingstock	As more vehicles are combined into a consist, the total possible grade may be reduced
Commuter rail	3%	These trains are not designed to climb high grades
Regional rail	3%	
Freight	1.5%	Typically higher grades make the freight service uneconomical, as more locomotives are needed
High speed rail	1.5%	Higher grades tend to have a large speed penalty
Monorails	6%	Able to climb fairly steep grades
Metros	3%	Steel on steel metros
Metros (rubber tyred)	12%	Very large grades can be accepted

A typical limit for a grade at a station is 1 in 100. Whilst larger grades can be accepted, it is generally preferable to limit grades at stations as much as possible.

REFERENCES

1. European Commission, *Tracks for Tilting Trains*, Fast and Comfortable Trains (D8), July 2005

2. Mancini, G. et al *New developments with the Italian solution for tilting trains: optimisation of tilting system on new generation of Pendolino trains*, www.uic.org/cdrom/2008/11_wcrr2008/pdf/R.2.4.3.5.pdf

3. Alessandro, E. New Developments for Tilting Trains, November 2001

4. Government of South Australia, Department of Planning Transport and Infrastructure, *PTSOM Code of Practice Volume 2, Track Geometry CP-TS-956*

5. Mochizuki, A. *JRTR Speed-up Story 2 Part 2: Speeding-up Conventional Lines and Shinkansen*, Japan Railway and Transport Review No 58 Oct 2011

6. Lindahl, M. *Track Geometry for high-speed railways*, Department of Vehicle Engineering Royal Institute of Technology, Stockholm 2001

7. Persson, R. *Tilting Trains Technology, benefits and motion sickness*, Thesis submitted to Royal Institute of Technology Stockholm, 2008

8. Forstberg, J. et al *Influence of different conditions for tilt compensation on symptoms of motion sickness in tilting trains*, Brain Research Bulletin, Vol 47, No 5, pp 525 – 535, 1998

Chapter 9 Signalling

Introduction

Signalling is the safety system that keeps trains apart and prevents them from colliding with each other. Signalling is one of the key engineering systems in for a railway. Signalling is often the system around which the safety case is built for a new railway.

There are many different types of signalling, some procedural, others based on engineering systems. Procedural systems, or systems that require the completion of forms and other administrative checks, are still common, although they are used on less thinly used lines, such as some freight lines.

It is always preferred for most professionals working on a railway to have an engineering system implemented for a railway, rather than rely upon something that needs the involvement of people. Time and time again, there have been many accidents where fully automatic signalling systems could have prevented accidents. The implementation of a fully operational signalling system is key to the management of a successful and safe railway.

That being said, in many cases a full signalling system is too expensive to implement. Alternatively, where a full signalling system (rather than a timetable based system for example) is implemented, railways have succumbed to the temptation to turn it off to achieve a higher headway, something that is done only with an increase in safety risk. It is best, where a signalling system is installed, to operate it correctly and not de-activate it to speed the passage trains.

The signalling system largely determines the headway. The headway is the minimum time between trains, and is a very important parameter for the performance of any railway. Lower headways are better, and cost more to install and maintain. The capacity of a rail system is strongly linked to the headway.

Below is a discussion of the "classic" method of structuring a signalling system, where the track is divided into blocks, and train occupation detected for each track section. This is a very common method of building a signalling system, and this will be discussed in some detail below. Automatic block signalling has the rail signals that has very recognisable signals, and this is still the most common method today of controlling the movement of trains.

Automatic Block Signalling

Automatic block signalling varies around the world, but one common theme is that there are signals that display a stop, a warning for the driver to slow his train down, and a signal indication that tells the driver he can proceed at full line speed. This arrangement is shown below for 3 aspect signalling:

The convention used in this document is shown below. Signals are drawn for three aspects as similar to traffic lights for cars and roads. In some railways, reds are at the bottom and greens at the top. In this book the British naming convention for the signals will be used, but recall that caution is called *"Approach"* in the US, and conceptually the two different indications are quite similar. The names of the indications are in the table below.

Aspects and Indications	
Colour	**Names**
Red	Stop
Yellow	Caution (Approach)
Green	Clear/Proceed

Three aspect signalling is often thought of as being the most basic and simple of signalling systems. For this reason, and because it is easy to explain how to calculate a headway, we start with a 3 aspect system over plain track.

A term used to describe indications is "restrictive". The most restrictive indication is stop, and the least restrictive is proceed. Caution is less restrictive than stop, but more restrictive than proceed.

Figure 9.1 Signals and Indications

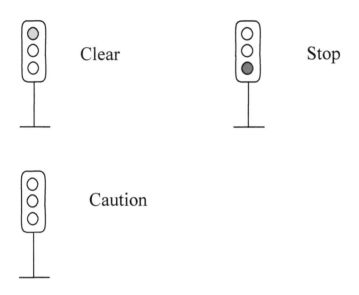

The track is divided up into "track sections", and each track section represents a small portion of the track. Track sections, normally, but not always, start and finish next to line side signals, and on a 1 kilometre section of track there may be one or several track sections. Engineering equipment is installed that allows for the detection of a train in any of these track sections. It is the occupancy of track section that is used for determining when trains can stop or proceed.

Figure 9.2 Track Sections

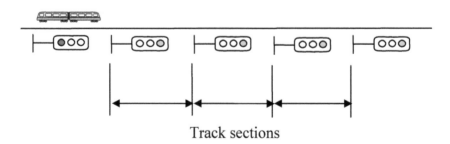

Track sections

The signalling system can detect if any or all of a train is in the track section. Even if only a small part of the train occupies the track section, the signalling system will know something is there. Within the track section, the track may be sub-divided into further small sections, depending on the capacity and signalling design. Within each of these subsections the signalling system cannot determine if the train is wholly within it, or just touching it at one point. A track section is commonly divided into two, but may be divided into many sub-sections.

The presence of the train changes the aspects and indications of the nearby signals, not for the ones in front of the train, but for the ones behind the train. As the train progresses in along the track the signals behind the train all go to stop, and then slowly change to less restrictive aspects once the train moves further forward. This is shown below, and once again note that it doesn't matter how much of the track section is occupied, as long as part of track section is occupied, then it is logically treated as occupied.

Figure 9.3 "Standard" operation of 3 Aspect Signals and Track Sections

Example 1

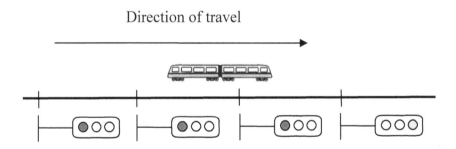

Example 2

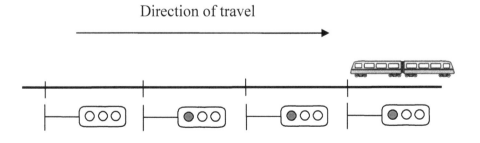

The signal to the rear of where the train is occupying the track shows a stop indication. It is often enough for one track section to be kept empty, and for three aspect signalling it is common to leave one track section empty at the rear of any train. It is possible to design the signalling system so that trains can close up much closer than that, but this type of signalling is more complex.

A clearing point is a place where, once a train moves past this point, then a signal clears to a higher indication. For the signal to move to a higher indication, the entire train must move past the clearing point. The clearance point is also often next to a signal, but there is no reason where it must be at a signal, and for track with overlaps the clearance point can be away from any signal.

The braking profile of any train determines the minimum spacing of signals. Signals can be very far apart, and where this is the case then headways can be quite high. In many cases railways will want to bring signals closer together, and there is a practical limit to how close together signals can be. All trains using a rail line must be able to stop, from full speed, between any two signals. Better brakes on trains, or lower speeds, means signals can be brought closer together.

It is important to distinguish between emergency braking and normal operational braking. For the calculations used here normal braking is used. Under normal conditions, the train will brake, and accelerate slowly, so that passengers are not thrown to the floor or stumble into other passengers. Emergency braking is used when an emergency situation arises, and the train must stop as quickly as possible. In an emergency it is expedient to stop much faster than normal, but rapid deceleration may mean passenger injuries, and in a bi-level train rapid deceleration may mean passengers may down stairs. It is better for the trains to decelerate rapidly than hit another train, as the damage from a collision will be far greater than hard braking. Emergency braking should only be used when absolutely necessary.

Older rollingstock often had very poor braking characteristics, and took a great distance to stop. In NSW there are anecdotal stories of some rollingstock where the braking deceleration was slower than the service deceleration, and so a driver that put his train into emergency braking may actually hit something ahead, which would not have happened had the driver used service braking. Whilst these stories are interesting, modern rollingstock generally has much better brakes than 50 years ago, and is able to stop relatively quickly. Trains are not buses, and can never stop as quickly as a vehicle with tyres (unless they have types themselves like some rubber tyre metros such as in Paris).

Beyond each signal is a clearing point which can be related to something called an overlap. To reduce the headways without increasing cost excessively, a concept called an overlap was introduced. An overlap is a section of track beyond a signal, which when a train passes it, clears a signal in the rear of the train. Overlaps distances are related to the speed that a train will stop under both emergency braking conditions, not normal conditions. This is shown in the diagram below.

Figure 9.4 Operation of Overlaps and Clearance Points

Example 1

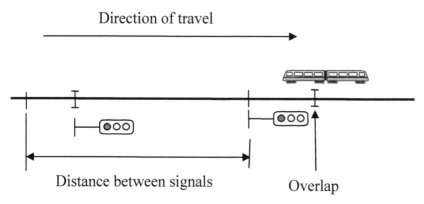

Example 2

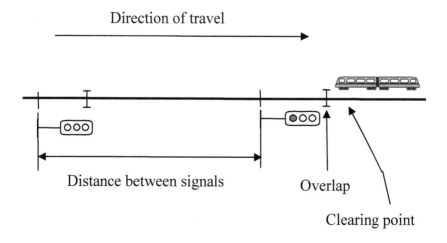

The signals shown above in example 1 are both at red because the rear of the train still occupies part of the overlap. Once the train passes beyond the overlap, then the first signal will clear to an aspect of yellow, or a meaning of "caution". Once a train clears an overlap then other trains are permitted into the track section past the signal to the rear of the train. Overlaps are a very cost effective way of reducing the headway, which means making it better, and are commonly used.

When a train passes a signal at stop (sometimes called a SPAD) the train needs to be prevented from continuing any further. Not all rail systems have such an installed system, but many do. Automatic train protection systems will perform this function, and on older rail systems there were devices called trainstops that can also perform this function. The overlap was intended to be the longest section of track that trains needed to stop, from line speed, under emergency conditions. The use of overlaps can reduce the headway, ie, make it better. Overlaps can be longer than track sections, and in higher aspect signalling the clearing point can be in very strange places. Calculations are included below for the situation where overlaps are installed, and not installed.

One important characteristic of the occupancy detection system, is that for most railways the system doesn't know what type of train is there. More modern ATP/ATO systems can detect which train is in what section, but most systems cannot. In addition, even if the section is only occupied by the last part of a train, this is the same as if the entire train is in that section. Partly occupying a section is the same as occupying most or all of the section.

The Special Case of 2 Aspect Signalling

Two aspect signalling is a very simple form of signalling, and there are only two possible indications in each signal, STOP, and CLEAR. It would seem to some that this type of signalling is the best, because it is the most simple. One significant problem with this type of signalling, is that it may not provide enough warning to drivers to stop their trains. Two aspect signalling can also have something called a distant signal, solves this problem, but adds others. Distant signals with 2 aspect signalling is discussed below.

Two aspect signalling is an interesting type of signalling that is rarely used in Australia, certainly for passenger networks. Its problems make its implementation difficult. It seems that 2 aspect signalling is common in some countries, such as Norway. Two aspect signalling may have a signal called a distant signal to warn drivers of the signal indications further ahead. Where there is no distant signal, the driver must stop before the first stop signal. Trains are not designed to stop quickly, and so a lot of warning is needed to stop a train. In practice a 2 aspect signal needs excellent sighting to allow a train to stop in time, or very low speeds.

Drivers need to see any stop signal before starting to stop, and of course there is a reaction time between when the signal is seen and when the train is instructed to start stopping, and braking begins. A single signal is all a driver will see in a two aspect system, and so the driver needs to be vigilant to begin braking as soon as the signal is seen.

The sighting distance in many railways is anywhere from 200 to 500 metres, although it can be much more in some cases. Where the track is long and straight, and there are no obstructions such as bridges or trees, then sighting can be over 1 km. In a metro system, where there are many curves, and tunnelled, and the tunnel is quite narrow, the farthest a driver can see might be only 200 metres. A more practical maximum speed for a two aspect system, with no other information provided to a driver about the signal indications ahead, is then somewhere around 50 to 80 kms/hr. This does not apply where there are distant signals, but where the system only contains mainline signals.

To mitigate this problem and provide additional time for the train to stop, a second signal is provided to warn the driver that there is a stop signal up ahead. The distant signal is used where the driver of the train would not be able to see the signal in time to stop, as in 2 aspect signalling there is no warning of the indication of the stop signal ahead. The distant signal is similar to a repeater signal, that gives the indication of another signal. A repeater signal is a signal that repeats the indication of a related signal in advance.

So we have the layout of 2 aspect signalling below. Distant signals show the indication of the mainline signal in advance of them, and nothing more. Distant signals usually do not show the same indication as the signal in advance, to avoid confusing the driver. Instead it is clear from the distant signal that it is providing information about the signal in advance.

Figure 9.5 Signalling Arrangement for 2 Aspect Signalling

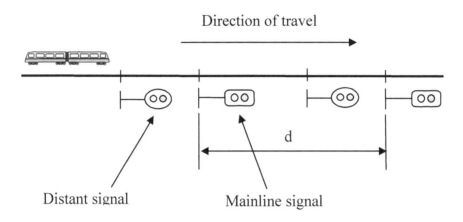

The figure below shows the operation of a distant signal. For a distant signal the most restrictive indication might be caution (approach), and the signal will be incapable of showing a red aspect. This is because there is a need not to confuse drivers with a false indication, that he should stop his train when he is not required to do so.

Figure 9.6 Distant Signals

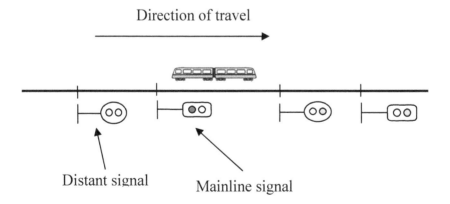

4 or more aspect signalling headways

Another common arrangement is 4 aspect signalling, where 4 different indications are possible in any one signal. This number of aspects has significantly better and lower headways than 3 aspect, and so is preferred for areas where the capacity needs to be high. Four aspect signalling is more complicated than 3, and so the explanation is a little more difficult.

The structure and layout of the signalling is shown below:

Figure 9.7 Four Aspect Signalling – no overlaps

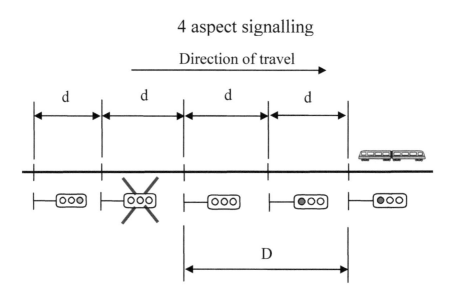

Introduced above is a new indication, a signal where the yellow light flashes. This is sometimes called "Medium", but in the US is also called "approach medium", although the rules are a little different in the UK for how this signal is treated. In the UK this aspect is known as "preliminary caution". There are a very large number of possible ways of displaying this aspect, and even in the same rail company there might be a number of different indications related to this aspect, and in Australia and NSW this is very much the case.

Notice that the stopping distance for trains is D, and it is permitted for a train stop over two signals for 4 aspect signalling, rather than from one to another as in 2 and 3 aspect signalling. This means that for 4 aspect signalling, a passenger train travelling at full speed, (and where there are no overlaps) where the driver does not respond to signals, the train may be unable to be stopped in time by any automatic system to prevent a collision with another train. In practice a driver almost never completely ignores signals, but incidents have been known to occur where drivers have driven their trains in such a way so that their trains has run almost 1 kilometre past the signal where the train should have stopped. Systems such as ATP are intended to stop this kind of problem, and work well to reduce the risk in this environment.

In some countries there is a real risk that a driver may pass multiple signals at stop, and collide with a train ahead. A common system to manage this is to have an aggressive system of monitoring the performance of drivers, and any driver that makes a mistake is taken off duty immediately. Constant filtering of the pool of drivers means that only vigilant drivers are allowed to drive, and the risk is dramatically reduced. This system, whilst cheap, has led to accidents.

Computer Assistance in Driving Trains, and ATP

Computers have been assisting with the driving of trains for over 40 years. The level of assistance provided to drivers varies dramatically depending on the type of system installed. Some systems provide almost no control over the driver's behaviour, others can drive the train without the driver at all. The greater the level of control the system has, potentially the lower the headway.

ATP stands for automatic train protection. ATP seems to be a very common term bandied about as a general term for any kind of computer assisted system that helps drive trains. A commonly held misconception is that an ATP system can drive a train automatically, this is not the case, and ATP system can be combined with an ATO system, but on its own an ATP system does not drive a train. ATP systems, the real ones, not the general term to apply to many different types of systems, seems to be the most commonly implemented, and so gets the most focus. A very popular version of ATP is ETCS, which stands for European Train Control System. ETCS is divided into a number of levels, which are very helpful for discussing ATP, and typical functionality of this type of system.

ATP systems operate differently from "standard" signalling systems, as drivers are provided with information significantly different from signals alongside the track. Drivers are provided with a current target speed, and a target speed for the end of the current track section. What a driver sees in an ATP system varies substantially from traditional lineside signalling.

A question that is often asked is the effect of introducing computer control to trains on the headway, and the reduction if any. At least in Australia a commonly held belief is that a computer can do better than a human driver in getting trains to slow down, stop, and then accelerate. A computer should be more consistent in the way trains are driven, and maybe might be able to reduce the headway. Is this the case? In some instances the answer to this question is yes, but in many cases it is no.

We should distinguish in cab signalling from ATP, although the two are often installed at the same time. In cab signalling is where the signals have been removed from beside the track, and a display incorporated into the driver's controls so that he can see what the signals would have displayed. In cab-signalling should not affect the headway in any significant way, unless it is installed at the same time as some other computer control system.

The three main types of computer assistance to trains is discussed. They are ATP, ATO, and ATS. Within ATP there are multiple levels, which are given numbers.

A/ Automatic train protection (ATP)

This system checks the speed of the driver and then corrects the speed by applying brakes. An ATP system does not cause a train to accelerate, but only decelerate. ATP systems do not drive trains, but instead provide train protection by braking the train. Either lineside equipment or train radio is used to supply trains with information on maximum permitted speeds.

ATP is particularly useful where trains move from one country to another, or from one railway to another, and the signals layout and design changes. As discussed above, the rules for signals and how they are read and what they mean change dramatically from one railway to another, and in Europe, trains that move across multiple countries may need to pass through several rail systems with different signal standards. Drivers, to travel through these different areas, would need to be trained and certified on each different system, and an ATP system can remove this requirement, allowing drivers certified on one system to drive through several railways. For this reason ATP is or will be installed in many different railways in Europe, to aid with harmonisation across the many different countries in the European Union.

One common version of ATP is ETCS, which is divided into 4 levels. The most basic system is level 0 or 1, and the most complex is level 3. The table below shows the different levels of ATP, and the type of speed checking they perform. This structure, with levels, is a convenient way of describing the different levels of complexity for an ATP system, but its use is not standard.

Levels of ATP/ETCS	
ATP Level	**Speed Checking**
0	Checks if a train can proceed at a signal, no speed control, other than the maximum speed permitted at the last balise. Usually applied for ETCS trains operating in non-ETCS areas.
1	A check of the speed and calculated speed profile at all points, but movement authority only checked at signals. Location calculated from the train wheels. Track still divided up into block sections
2	Train in constant contact with ATP system through radio, movement authorities updated as train moves through block section, maximum train speed calculated at all points. Interlocking still using blocks, not moving block.
3	Moving block calculation of the position of trains and braking curves. The authority for a train to move is determined from the performance of the train, and a braking curve that extends from the front of the train.

Level 3 ATP is considered to be the "Holy Grail" of signalling, as train movements are not based on fixed block sections but on a calculation of the distance to the next train and speed. Moving block systems have a much lower headway, which is highly desirable. Note that with most moving block systems (at least as far as the author is aware), the braking curve calculation is made on the basis that the train ahead is stationary and not moving. Factoring in the movement of the train ahead is something that currently is not offered as part of an ATP level 3 system.

Level 2 ATP does not change the official headway, as the block sections and interlocking calculations do not change. Where overlaps are installed, then there may be a small change in the headway, as overlaps can be reduced in size. For headways where trains are running on restricted aspects, the headway may reduce, as the train is constantly in contact with the signalling system. It is possible that the signal may change for a train, after is has passed the signal that displays something other than a full proceed indication.

Where a rail line is designed fresh with ATP level 2, then it is possible to improve the headway, and increase the line capacity. Most track sections are composed of a number of smaller track sub-sections, in which trains can be detected. With ATP level 2 it is possible to have a "virtual" signal for each track circuit, something that would be very expensive with traditional signalling. This allows the creation of a signalling system with a large number of aspects, where a reduction in headway is possible. This is not possible where ATP is retro-fitted to an existing signalling system, as the design of the system will not allow this to occur, unless of course a lot of money is spent.

ATP is often attractive to install because of the reduction in lineside signalling equipment. Level 2 and 3 of ETCS allow the elimination of many common infrastructure items. Not only does this save cost, but the risk to employees of the rail maintainer is reduced as there is a reduced need to access track. This benefit should always be compared to the capital cost for the construction and implementation of any new system.

The consensus (at least in Australia) with ATP level 1 & 2 is that these systems only marginally change the headway of any signalling system. The main reason why the headway does not change is because the track sections do not change, and the underlying signalling system remains the same. Also in practice drivers rarely accelerate and decelerate frequently, but prefer the set the speed for the train and then to coast along on one speed setting. If a driver sees an yellow signal, but then the ATP system changes this signal to green, the driver will know that as he approaches the next signal that it will once again display a yellow signal, and he will have to slow down again. This constant speeding up and slowing down, in theory will yield faster trains with reduced headways, but in practice little will change because drivers just don't do this. Drivers are familiar with the timetable, and will know what train is ahead and its stopping pattern, and adjust the speed on their train to suit.

B/ Automatic train operation (ATO)

Automatic train operation (ATO) is when a computer drives the train. The train may or may not have someone in the front of the train, and this person may only operate doors and make announcements, rather than actually drive the train. In this case the driver of the train is sometimes referred to as an "operator". With ATO some of the functions of the train may be performed manually, such as opening and closing doors, or all functions may be fully automated.

ATO can dramatically reduce the time taken to turn around trains at a terminus. Most rail lines have a terminus at either end, unless they are loops, and so when the train reaches the terminus then it needs to stop, and change direction. The driver needs to close up the driver's cabin, complete a checklist of small tasks, and then walk to the other end of the train and commence driving from that end. The time taken to walk from one end of the train to another is about a couple of minutes, plus potentially a toilet break, and so the turnaround time for a "normal" train is often around 5 minutes. ATO systems do not require drivers, so the turnaround time is very minimal.

As the turnaround time is low, in some cases this may result in a lower headway. At a terminus station, trains often change direction whilst sitting on a platform, and when this occurs then the normal time is required for drivers to compete all their tasks and change ends. In some cases it is possible for trains to change direction from either platform, then the minimum headway can be very low, as there are two platforms to turnaround trains rather than one. If for some reason trains can only change direction from one platform rather than both platforms, then an ATO system can be invaluable in getting trains in and out of the terminus quickly.

ATO does not necessarily include a system that allows a remote operator to see the movement of trains on a computer screen. The ATO system just controls the movement of the train, and does not necessarily have a system that communicates what is happening back to a control centre. This function is called ATS and is discussed below.

The author has read documents that state that there is an ATO system that does not change the headway. However, some improvements are possible, and small changes in the headway are possible with an ATO system, and this is because:
- Trains accelerate more evenly, and the variation associated with driver behaviour is removed.
- As trains are now computer controlled, acceleration and deceleration can be a little higher, as the computer the calculate the rate of acceleration and deceleration precisely
- Trains can potentially enter a station at normal speed, and then brake evenly to the end of the platform, when the virtual signal at the end of the platform would show a red indication. This is in contrast to a real

driver would probably could only enter a station at "normal" speed when the signal at the end of the platform shows an indication lower than a red.

The author's experience of ATO trains has been that the acceleration was very smooth, and that an increase in average acceleration is possible. ATO allows for better ride comfort, and human driven trains can have much rougher acceleration. Driverless trains can be very difficult to implement on freight systems.

C/ Automatic train supervision (ATS)

Automatic train supervision is a computer and software system that collects and manages information on the movement of trains, and the other systems that also control the movement of train, listed above, which are ATP and ATO. Both of these systems can operate without anyone in a control centre viewing the movement of trains (except for emergencies and out-of-course events, of course). The ATS system allows the creation of a "flight control" for trains, where rail staff can sit and monitor how the railway is performing. Typically, the function of an ATS system includes:

- Monitoring train punctuality
- Providing alarms if anything untoward happens (such as a broken rail, equipment failure, etc...)
- Allows visualisation of the status of the rail network and where trains are positioned
- Allows for operators of the ATS system to intervene and change the operation of the network

ATS does not change the headway of a train system. This system only allows the viewing of the movement of trains, and does not change the way the headway and braking curves are calculated.

REFERENCES

1. Wardrop, A and Suess, P, *Strategies to Increase Line Capacity and Reduce Travel Time in a Mixed Passenger and Freight Corridor*, The Institution of Railway Signal Engineers Inc Australasian Section Incorporated, Nov 2009

2. Vincze, B. & Tarnai, G. *Development and Analysis of Train Brake Curve Calculation Methods with Complex Simulation*, Budapest University of Technology and Economics.

3. Landex, A. & Schittenhelm, B. & Kaas A.H. & Schneider-Tilli, J *Capacity measurement with the UIC 406 capacity method*, Computers in Railways XI, 2008

4. Kruegar, H. *Parametric Modeling in Rail Capacity Planning*, Proceedings of the 1999 Winter Simulation Conference

5. Murphy, E. *The Application of ERTMS/ETCS Systems*, IRSE Technical Convention Melbourne, Oct 2007

6. Emery, D. *Reducing the headway on high-speed lines*, 9th Swiss Transport Research Conference Sept 2009

7. Moore, T. *Understanding Signalling Overlaps*, IRSE Technical Meeting: Sydney, March 2011

8. Huth, P. *Overview of QR Signalling Principles*, IRSE Technical Meeting, Brisbane, July 2008

9. Kerr, D. Rail Signal Aspects and Indications, http://dougkerr.net/Pumpkin/articles/Rail_signal_aspects.pdf

10. Van Breusegem, V. et al *Traffic Modeling and State Feedback Control for Metro Lines*, IEEE Transactions on Automatic Control, Vol 36, No 7, July 1991

11. Union Internationale Chemin de Fer *Capacity*, UIC Code 406, June 2004

12. Kerr, D. *Rail Signal Aspects and Indications*, Issue 3, March 2007, http://dougkerr.net/Pumpkin/articles/Rail_signal_aspects.pdf

Chapter 10 Stabling

Stabling is where trains are stored, often at night, and sometimes during the day when they are not used. Passenger trains are commonly stabled during the day between peak periods. The reader will probably note the similarity between trains and horses, because the same words are used to describe both. Stabling is very important for any operational railway, as trains often need to be stabled, and the location of stabling can dramatically affect how trains are scheduled to move throughout the network.

Stabling facilities need to be distinguished from maintenance and maintenance centres, and they are quite different. Trains are not normally stabled in maintenance centres, as these have limited space, and far more space is needed for stabling of trains than is normally available in maintenance centres. Maintenance centres may be able to store a small number of trains, but ordinarily trains are stored in large stabling yards. It is also common for stabling to be co-located with maintenance centres, 20 or 30 metres away, or trains may need to pass through the stabling to get to the maintenance centre.

Stabling yards are not pretty things, and while rail transport is sexy and good to look at, stabling yards are ugly. Full of tracks, cluttered with trains, and with a very industrial look and feel, many stabling yards are very unsightly. In many cases cities with large stabling yards near the centre of the city have moved them away just to avoid having to look at them, or hide them so that no one can see them. In Melbourne much of the stabling available in the centre of the city has been removed, as it was considered a terrible eyesore. Likewise, for the tram depot in Hong Kong, it is superbly well hidden, and it's not a pretty thing, but it is well hidden. The larger the stabling yard, the worse this problem seems to be.

Given the poor visual appearance of a stabling yard, they are often hidden away as best as possible. This might be achieved by walls, or other structure that hides the yard. Alternatively, the yard may by sandwiched between two other rail lines, so that no one can see it through the other trains. Alternatively, it may be hidden in a place where there are no people to be affected by its poor appearance.

The problem is a little less serious for the various forms of light rail, such as trams, light rail proper, and Automated People Movers (APMs). These smaller trains can be tucked away in places where they cannot be seen, or buildings can be used to house all the vehicles. Larger trains, such as HSR trains, or commuter trains, will be difficult to hide, and the stabling yards will be large. Freight yards are truly enormous, and are extremely difficult to hide. Freight yards are just dreadful, and noisy, and should be put in industrial areas where no one lives nearby.

The picture below is of a tram depot in Brunswick in Melbourne. This photo was taken around lunchtime so the depot is almost empty. Tram depots are a type of stabling, and unusually for rail transport, trams can be stored inside under cover when stabled.

Tram Depot in Melbourne

Stabling yards are often a maintenance problem, and require a lot of maintenance compared to plain track. Where large numbers of trains are stabled, there needs to be a corresponding large amount of infrastructure to accommodate the trains, and this means a high concentration of infrastructure in a stabling yard. The cost of installing stabling can be substantial, especially where the number of trains to be stabled is very large. Given the quantity of infrastructure, there are constant failures of the engineering equipment, such as points and track circuits, so maintenance crews will need to be stationed very close to a stabling yard to ensure any failures are fixed quickly.

A common problem with older railways it seems is that there seems to be stabling all throughout their networks. A reasonable amount of stabling is very desirable, but too much of it can be a problem. Putting stabling everywhere is very attractive for operators of railways, because it provides all sorts of operational flexibility; if a train breaks down then it can be quietly stored in a stabling yard somewhere until it can be moved to a maintenance centre to be repaired. There are many advantages to having stabling everywhere, and operators of rail systems may ask for lots of stabling to be installed, even when there already is quite a lot. From a maintenance and cost perspective it's a real problem, and stabling yards should be installed only where needed.

Stabling needs to be properly designed and installed to allow the most efficient operation of any railway. Stabling is important, and where it is installed in the wrong place, or poorly designed, then operational railways can face some serious problems. Some of the problems with poorly designed or located stabling includes:

- Trains need to be moved large distances to start their runs in the morning, or finish at night in poor places, and again need to be moved
- Stabling can't accommodate all the trains that operate on a line, and only some can be stabled
- Infrastructure in the stabling yard is in poor condition, as the yard is so busy that important maintenance cannot be performed
- The stabling yard is too large for the number of trains stored there, and much of the equipment is not used, and is rusting away
- The stabling yard is in a place that is difficult to access, and far away from where maintenance staff are based
- Entry and exit from the stabling yard is a bottleneck, and the stabling yard cannot put trains into and receive trains from the network quickly enough
- Stabling is not long enough to accommodate the length of trains that are needed

Overall stabling yards are quite important. The author's observation is that a significant percentage of rail transport projects seem to either be about stabling, or involve changes to stabling. It is possible for a rail line to be designed to handle large numbers of trains, but the stabling is inadequate to meet the needs of the rail line.

Much consideration should be given to the placement of stabling yards. Stabling yards may be located where land is available, and this might be well away from where trains start operating and finish for the night. This can create large problems, as trains are moving around all the time, to get back to a place where they can be stabled. Moving trains from poorly placed stabling yards is expensive, staff need to staff early to get trains into position, there are the power costs and wear and tear on the train, and it makes the maintenance window for track smaller, as there are many train movements before the start of train services.

Another common problem is the entrance to and exit from stabling. It is a common problem for the capacity into and out of the stabling to be insufficient. Where this is the case, the stabling yard is limited in how many trains can be managed, regardless of its actual size. Resolving this problem can be difficult, as enlarging the entrance to the stabling can often be a difficult thing to achieve. Land, and the lack of it, can be the problem.

Freight is stabled, but it's a bit different from passenger services. Freight locomotives can be coupled to many different types of freight wagons, and when not being used these need to be stored somewhere. Some freight wagons may be very infrequently used, and spend most of their time sitting in some freight yard somewhere. The long term storage of different freight wagons is not normally called stabling, but rather just storage in the yard. Nonetheless it is a type of stabling. .

For trains with dedicated locomotives, when the train drives into any kind of stabling, or for that matter a terminus, the question arises as to how to get the locomotive out again. Locomotives can move in reverse, and entire trains can be propelled backwards if needed, but it's always better to put a locomotive at the front of the train rather than the rear. It is possible to put a second track next to the first to allow the locomotive to get out from behind the train, and sometimes this is a called a run-around road. EMU's do not have this problem, and can normally be driven from both ends of the train. Turntables were once common, and these are a way of turning locomotives around. In some situations there may be an electric locomotive pulling coaches which are unpowered, and one solution to this problem is to put an electric locomotive at each end of the train. Otherwise, just like diesel locomotives, the locomotive will need to be moved from one end of the train to the other.

As part of the asset management of any railway there needs to be continuous removal of any surplus assets, and stabling is a perfect place to do this. Over time the operational need of the railway changes, and stabling yards are often full of old disused equipment, and so an asset removal program can be useful in removing unwanted equipment. Removing old rusting equipment is often not done, because the equipment costs very little to upkeep when it is not used, but the number of asset items of disused equipment can build up quite quickly. Whilst this book is not really about asset management, it's not really good to let the amount of disused equipment build up to the point where there is more equipment not used than actually used, and this seems to be common, at least in Australia.

So how is a stabling yard described? The key parameters for a stabling yard are:

- The number of tracks (sometimes called roads, even though it a rail track) which can be used to stable trains
- The length of the stabling tracks
- The number of trains that can be stabled. This is normally the number of tracks that can be used for stabling, but sometimes these numbers will be different
- The number of trains that can enter and exit the stabling yard per hour. It is entirely possible for a stabling yard to possess an exit through which it can take hours to get all the trains out
- The expected used capacity of the stabling yard, and this can be a number anywhere between 0 to 100%. It seems normal that for any new stabling that almost all the capacity would be used, but for old ones the percentage used might be close to zero.
- The type of train that can be stabled, electric, diesel, or even steam. Stabling for diesel trains often requires fuel pumps, where trains can be refuelled with diesel. Steam trains require water for the boiler, and often sand, and these need to be available.
- The availability of decanting. Long distance trains have toilets, and the effluent needs to be removed from the train. Old style trains did not store their effluent, but thankfully most all these trains have been removed from service around the world.
- The availability of water to add to any water tanks on trains (used for flushing toilets, drinking water for passengers, etc).

A quick point should be made here; refuelling trains and adding water is not something done only in a maintenance centre. Maintenance is performed at a frequency normally around months, ie, 3 months, and this far too long to add water only at these times. Whilst it may be possible to add water to a train at a maintenance centre, normally this would be done where trains are stabled. There is no reason why a maintenance centre should not have these facilities, but removing effluent from a train needs to be done almost daily, and this is far too frequent to be done at a maintenance centre.

The calculation of the total capacity of the yard is normally pretty easy, but the number of trains that can be moved in and out is a bit harder. Speeds in stabling yards are normally limited, and 25 kms/hr seems to be common, at least in Australia. Capacity into and out of a stabling yard is often limited when there are only two tracks in and out. Where only one track is available into and out of a yard, problems with entry and exit can be even more severe.

Tram depots are an interesting form of stabling, because of the short length of trams, tram depots are often covered. Very large numbers of trams can be stored in one place, because trams are short in length, and are narrower than most trains. As mentioned above, tram depots can often be hidden because of their small size.

The photo below is of a turntable, and this is where train locomotives where turned around. Little used now, turntables were once very common. The way a turntable works is that a locomotive is driven onto the turntable, and then the turntable rotates so that the locomotive faces the opposite direction. Turntables are essentially a giant circle, with a movable section of track in the middle. In NSW at least turntables were often hand powered, and railway staff would turn a handle, and in so doing the turntable would spin around slowly.

Locomotive turntable

Most turntables were in stabling yards, so that the carriages or wagons of the steam train would be decoupled from the locomotive, and the steam engine would be turned around, and the reconnected to the carriages, and then move off in the opposite direction from whence it came. Very old staling yards may still have turntables in them, especially where old steam trains are occasionally used for heritage and tourist purposes.

The Tidal Nature of Commuter Services

Recall that commuter services are a special type of rail system, which specialise in moving people to their place of work, particularly on weekdays. The structure of commuter services is relatively standard, passengers are moved from outlying suburbs to a central location, usually where businesses are located. These businesses are often offices, and need office workers to staff them. Shift work is rare with offices, so there is little need for rail services outside of business hours. Office work is mostly day work, Monday to Friday, so many workers are needed during these times.

Commuter services are markedly different from metro style services, which operate throughout the day, and may have a higher service frequency during the day, but do not stop operation. Some of the key differences between a commuter service and a metro style service, or light rail for that matter, are:

- Some stations will close once the peak period has ended
- Trains operating in the peak are very crowded, and those that operate outside the peak are much more lightly loaded, or even almost empty
- The demand for passenger services is towards the centre of the city in the morning, and away from the centre of the city in the afternoon
- Rail services may cease away from peak periods
- There are direct services on a line to a city centre of business district in peak, but away from this passengers need to change trains to get to a city centre

In any city with a significant number of corporations operating in a large business district, there are normally rail services that cater for the employees of these businesses. Rail services start early in the morning, and then run throughout the peak period, and then resume in the afternoon when people want to go home. Commuter services have a reduced service between peak periods, or potentially no service at all. In some cases services only operate at certain times of the day. Alternatively services from the CBD to any extremely large regional centre may continue 24 hours a day, if the demand is there to justify it.

Train movements, especially for commuter and regional services are tidal. What this means is that in the morning trains move from the outskirts of a big city into the middle in the morning, and in the afternoon, when city workers finish work, trains move from the centre of the city to the outskirts or regional centres. So trains start their morning in a rural or regional stabling yard, and then move to some central point, where they are stabled again, waiting for the office workers to complete their day, and then move out again. In this situation there will be two stabling yards at least, one at the end of the line at the regional centre, and then another in centre of the large city. Train movements are tidal because they all move together in a daily pattern, much like a tide.

So how is all of this relevant to stabling? Well as there are more services into the city centre rather than out, trains accumulate in the centre of the city, and then in the afternoon these trains are needed, to move passengers from the CBD out to the suburbs again. This means that there is a requirement for stabling yards in the centre of the city, to accommodate these trains, and them some more stabling yards at the end of several rail lines to accommodate these commuter trains at night. Stabling does not necessarily need to be provided, but where it isn't there will be large numbers of empty train movements, which cost money to make.

Well designed stabling

The ease of use of any stabling yard is another important consideration. Well designed stabling, in addition to having plenty of capacity, located in the correct place, and having the ability to get trains in and out quickly, also needs to be designed so that rail employees can use it efficiently. Drivers need to be able to quickly and efficiently get into and out of trains. There should be toilets and other facilities available. There are many problems with stabling that has either been poorly designed, or has some kind of problem that makes it hard to use. Some of these problems include:

- The lighting is very poor and driver and train staff cannot see where to walk when they are getting in and out of trains
- The ground is uneven and train staff can trip or fall over when walking to or from trains
- Access is difficult into and out of the stabling yard
- The stabling has some environmental factor that impacts upon its function as a stabling yard, such as being located near the ocean and sea spray washes up onto the train
- The stabling yard is located in a high crime area and drivers and train staff get attacked going to and from their trains
- Fencing is inappropriate for the stabling yard
- Toilets are inadequate or too far away
- Other staff amenities are not available

Fencing is quite important for any stabling, as vandals commonly spray paint trains in yards. The experience in Australia has been that the location where trains are stabled needed to have substantial fencing to prevent vandalism, and 2.5 metre high fences are common, with razor wire on top of the fence. This level of security is necessary to prevent a lot of damage to trains.

Different Configurations of Stabling

One of the most important features of any stabling is the entry and exit. Stabling needs to be large enough to accommodate all the trains that are stabled there, but most passenger rail networks have a peak period in the morning, and it is necessary to get trains in and out quickly from the stabling yard onto the running lines. Many different types of entry and exit into a stabling yard exist, but most of them have severe limits on the throughput of trains in and out. The schematics below demonstrate this.

In the layout below the stabling is shown as purple, and the running lines in black. The configuration below is very common, and trains need to move from the running lines to get into the stabling yard. There is only one entrance into and out of the stabling yard, so this is a strong limitation on the number of trains that can enter and exit the stabling yard, nothwithstanding the small size of the yard.

Figure 10.1 Single Entry Stabling Yard

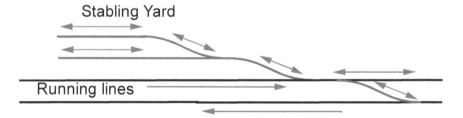

The stabling yard below is larger than the one above, and has two entrances and exits into the yard. Trains will be able to enter and leave more quickly than the one above. Also note that trains leaving the stabling yard to go to the bottom running line will need to cross one of the running lines to get there, and this movement may cause operational problems, and interfere with the passage of other trains. However, despite this, it is clear that this layout is superior to the one above.

Figure 10.2 Multiple Entry Stabling Yard

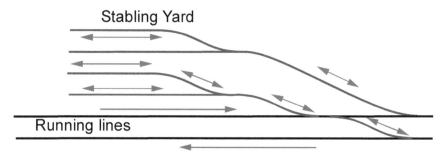

The above layout allows for something called parallel moves, where trains can move in and out of the yard at the same time. This layout is better when large numbers of trains need to be moved in and out of the yard quickly.

The layout below has stabling at the end of the running lines, and they run out and are replaced with a stabling yard. This type of layout can be very efficient, because trains can have direct access to the running lines.

Figure 10.3 Stabling at the End of the Rail Line

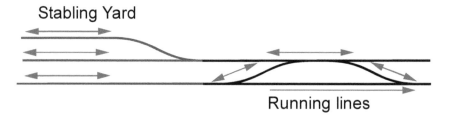

Interestingly a review of the stabling yards in and around Sydney shows that this layout, despite many advantages, is very uncommon. In practice this type of stabling can only be implemented where the rail line ends, and the stabling yard is put at the end of this line. Many rail lines, especially for regional, commuter and intercity services do not end, but continue past the terminus to another destination.

The schematic below shows how stabling is often designed in practice. In the schematic below there is a terminus on the left, where trains arrive and depart from. The terminus is the end of the rail line, and the tracks do not continue any further than this. There is often a high value location just located past the end of the rail terminus, and the railway cannot be built up or continued any further.

Figure 10.4 Terminus and Stabling

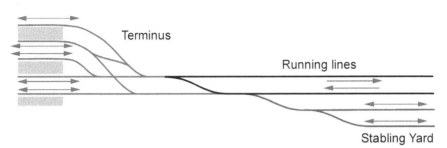

On the right hand side is the stabling, which is located further back away from the terminus. Trains arriving and departing from the terminus will pass alongside the stabling, and the number of tracks will appear, to passengers, to be quite large. This layout is quite common, as it has the advantage that trains, after completing their revenues service, can be moved back into the stabling yard to be stored, and then retrieved when needed. The presence of the stabling increases the effective capacity of the terminus, and more trains can terminate in the terminus. When the terminus becomes full, trains can be moved from the terminus to the stabling yard very quickly. Also, if there is a problem with a train, it can be brought in to the terminus, passengers taken off, and then moved into the stabling yard to await repair. The usefulness of this layout is the key reason why it's so common.

Unfortunately it is a very ugly layout, and aesthetically very unappealing. As the terminus is almost always located next to a city centre, them the stabling yard will also be located on high value land.

In some cases the running lines are so busy that stabling needs to be accessed through a dive, or possibly a flyover. What is shown in the figure below is a dive, but essentially the concept is the same for flyover. Trains need to get from either track into the stabling yard, and there is a desire to avoid an at grade crossing, so the track needs to pass either under or over the running lines.

The layout below shows a dive combined with a stabling yard. The stabling will almost always need to be on one side or the other of the running lines, so one of the lines will need to cross to the other side. In this case it is the lower line that needs to cross to the stabling yard, and it does so through a dive. A dive is a rail tunnel that dips down below the track and then comes up again on the other side.

Figure 10.5 Stabling Accessed through a Dive

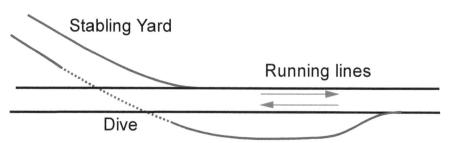

One problem with dives is that they fill up with water. Being the lowest point in the rail system, much of the water from rain and seepage makes its way into a dive. Dives, unless they are in an area that has almost no rain at all, will need a pumping station to remove all the water. Once water makes its way into a tunnel it becomes the responsibility of the railway, and this may mean cleaning and processing the water.

A flyover performs the same function as a dive but goes over the track rather than under. Both require a lot of space and are expensive to build. Once constructed the maintenance cost is quite small. Railways tend to avoid dives and flyovers, given the cost of construction, but they are very effective.

Note that flyovers and dives are used to get rail vehicles into and out of stabling, yards, and maintenance centres more efficiently. They allow trains to pass over or under the running lines without interfering with the movement of trains on the running lines. They are clearly the best way to get trains in and out of stabling yards, but are expensive.

Stabling of Freight

Freight trains need to be stabled like any other train, but freight stabling is a little different to stabling for passenger trains. Some of the differences are:
- Freight trains are very long, often over 1 km, and sometimes over 2 kms, so any stabling for freight will be very long and large
- Freight trains are rarely electric and so this large freight yard will usually have no overhead or electric traction power (although there are exceptions)
- Many freight wagons are only occasionally used, and this often sit in a freight yard waiting to be used, and may be covered in rust. In Australia milk wagons are rarely used, but milk was commonly

transported by rail, so there are many surplus wagons sitting idle in various freight yards

- Freight locomotives will need to refuel, so there will often be refuelling facilities in the yard
- Very large freight yards will sometimes have other freight facilities around them, such as road freight terminals. For large freight yards with a lot of traffic, the combined road rail freight terminals can cover a very large area
- As rail freight often only generates a small profit, any freight yard are often in poor condition and covered with weeds. Coal freight yards are the exception and are almost always in good condition because of the much higher profitability of selling coal (at least in Australia)

The diagram below shows how freight may be stabled. The running lines move around a long freight yard, and the stabling yard can be entered from either end. Note that stabling yards are often more complex than this, and the yard drawn below is a bit simplified.

Figure 10.6 Freight Stabling Yard

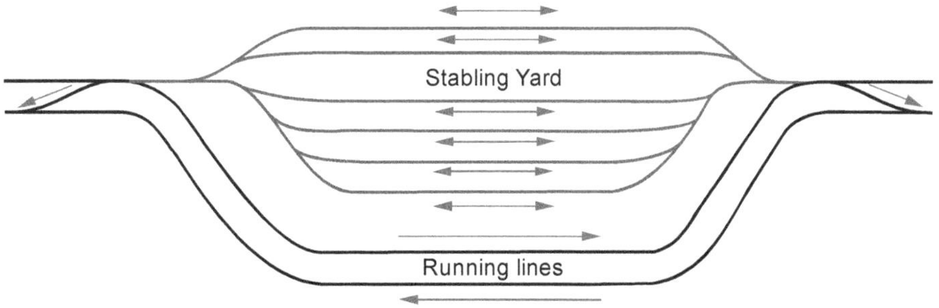

This type of stabling is suitable for long freight trains. The yard show above can be extremely large, and over 1 kilometre long. Also trains can enter from either end, have wagons added or removed, and locomotives added or removed, and then can enter or exit from either end. In many ways this layout is very suitable for freight, particularly for intermodal traffic, or any other freight where freight trains are marshalled.

Chapter 11 Underground Tunnels & Stations

Underground rail lines are a common feature of many rail systems. Tunnelling a rail line has many advantages, as the rail system can avoid obstacles above ground, and pass effortlessly through major cities and under mountains. Tunnelling a rail line often means have underground stations as well, and underground stations require care in their construction to ensure that they meet the needs of any rail system.

Putting a rail line underground dramatically increases the cost of constructing it. Much more infrastructure is needed for an underground station and rail line, and the entire system gets much more complex and difficult to manage. From a design perspective, tunnelling a rail line is challenging, and requires many more engineers and highly skilled specialists to build correctly.

Underground stations need to be designed to minimise any fire related risks to passengers. Any smoke evolved from a station can potentially accumulate there and injure or kill anyone who cannot be evacuated. Care must be exercised in the design of any station to ensure it is correctly designed, and does not create and safety or passenger movement problems.

Many different facilities can be installed in stations to improve amenity, and an underground station requires more of these than a comparable above ground stations. As radio signals from communications companies will not be able to penetrate underground, as part of the construction a communications system to relay mobile phone calls may be needed. Typically many communications systems become more challenging in an underground environment. Ventilation too may need to be provided, especially for a deep station.

An important decision to make is the staffing level at the station, is a station required to have staff all the time, or not at all? In large commuter and regional systems, as well as tram systems, many stations are not staffed, and there is often no booking office or facilities for station staff to work. It is possible for one side of a station to be staffed, and the other not. Commonly many stations are only staffed during certain times. The choice of staffing level, and especially if the station is staffed at all, will influence what structures are built on the station.

The time a train spends at a station is called the dwell. In this US the term layover is used to describe the time a train spends at a station. The management of dwell times is a key part of successful station design. Heavy overcrowding of stations can result in increases in headway, as trains are delayed waiting for passengers to board and alight. One of the objectives of station design is to minimise dwell times. Underground stations can be very cramped, as excavation costs money, and stations are much cheaper to build if they are smaller. Some underground stations have very thin platforms, and so dwell times may be severely effected by the design of the station. In serious cases, such as in Sydney, train headways and overall system capacity may be degraded.

The question arises of what exactly constitutes an underground station. A station may be partially underground, and be built on a hill or cutting, so that it appears to be underground, or may be partially underground. Stations can have shopping centres built over them, so that they appear to be underground, but actually are above or at ground level. In some cases a station may be constructed at the top of a hill, and so is underground, but at each end of the station is a portal where the rail line moves out from underground, and so the only part of the rail line that is underground is the station. In Sydney Kings Cross station is designed this way, where at each end of the station there is a portal, and the rail line at both ends of the station is above ground.

Whilst a search for any references failed to reveal anything that discussed what the definition for an underground station is, the following observations can be made:
- Stations located deep underground will always be defined as being underground
- Stations where the rail line is buried for some distance either side of the station can be considered as being underground
- Stations which are above ground, but covered by a shopping centre, can in some cases be considered to be an underground station, especially where the rail lines at either end of the station are also underground
- Elevated stations, which are above ground, may appear to the travelling public to be below ground, but should always considered above ground stations
- Stations with one or more sides exposed, which are not walls or tunnels, are clearly not underground stations
- Any station where a passenger can look up and see the sky, without looking through a roof or other structure is probably not an underground station

Perhaps the best rule to use is if, from any part of the station it is impossible for any passenger standing on a platform to see natural sunlight, for any part of the day, then the station can be considered to be an underground station. Applying this rule would exclude a large number of stations, such as Taoyuan station in Taiwan, on the high speed rail system, where sunlight is clearly visible at one end of the station for most of the day. It is suggested that the definition for underground stations be interpreted fairly strictly, so as to limit the number of stations defined as being underground.

Ordinarily freight trains are not permitted to pass through underground stations that service passengers. The mixing of freight and passenger services has a profound effect on the design of any rail line, and this is especially so for underground stations and rail lines. Freight trains are often diesel fuelled, and this is a combustible fuel, and even though it is difficult for it to catch fire, it will under the right circumstances. Diesel motors can explode if poorly maintained, so extreme care must be taken if freight trains are permitted through underground stations. Often freight will be banned from passing through any underground rail station with passengers, but potentially in some cases it may be required to allow freight to pass through underground station. An alternative solution may be to restrict the freight trains to particular times of the day when passenger trains do not operate. In Australia there are no underground stations where freight is permitted to pass through at all.

Another consideration with underground stations is how to manage passengers when they become ill. This seems to be more and more common lately, certainly in Australia where the population is aging, and passengers can become ill on trains and then be moved from the train to the platform. Underground stations can be so deep below ground that it may be difficult or near impossible to get passengers out when they become ill. This is especially the case for stations with no lifts, which is not uncommon, even for underground stations. Some passengers can be very heavy, and not that easy to remove or assist from the station, so some care needs to be exercised in deciding how to get ill passengers from platforms. We can also note that almost all stations will not have a lift operating from the unpaid surface to paid platforms deep below ground, and so as a minimum 2 lifts are needed to get an ill passenger to the surface to be met by an ambulance. The need to be able to evacuate sick passengers is a complication to the fire and life safety design required for stations.

Fire Protection and Safety for Underground Stations

Underground stations are an enclosed and confined space. If a fire starts in an underground station then the smoke can accumulate very rapidly, and present an extremely serious risk to anyone still in the station. Smoke can rapidly accumulate and cause damage to the lungs of anyone present, and so smoke management is an important part of station design.

Large fires in an underground station are very serious. Apart from the risk of the smoke, what can make fires so dangerous is the speed with which they can grow. Small fires can become large fires very quickly if there is enough material and oxygen. The fast growth rates of fires means that once a fire starts there is very little time to evacuate passengers from both rollingstock or from platforms, and designing stations to allow rapid egress is very important.

The main defence against fires in underground stations is removing any possible fuel source. Materials used in the construction of a station should be highly resistant to catching fire, and not burn unless heated to a very high temperature. All materials will burn if the temperature is high enough, so it is not possible to find a material that is completely resistant to fire. Fire resistant materials should also be resistant to structural collapse as long as possible when exposed to a fire, and the longer the better. Structural collapse in an underground station would be very serious were it to ever happen.

In the construction of any station, fire hardening is very important, and it will be mandated in the design. National and international standards are often quite strict on the materials to be used in any station, especially an underground one, and so it is safe to assume in most cases that stations will be fire hardened. Other mitigations for fires in underground stations include escape and exit from the station, and whilst not as important as fire hardening the station and rollingstock, and also not as important as stopping the fire starting in the first place, it also important and needs to be considered.

Electrical wiring in a station also needs to be a very good quality, as fire can start when problems occur in the wiring. Electricity has the capability, especially where the cabling has short circuits or bare wiring, to start fires. To protect against this special wiring is used that is more fire resistant, and less likely to fray or become bare and have the potential to start a fire.

Large fires are fortunately very rare in almost all modern rail systems. Small fires are commonly started by vandals and school children as pranks, and can be quite common. To prevent these minor incidents becoming very major, it is important for any rail system to ensure that fire hardened materials are used in stations and for rollingstock. A small fire started by an 11 year old school student should never be allowed to become a raging inferno, and the use of poor quality materials can allow this to happen.

An important standard for the design of stations is NFPA 130, Standard for Fixed Guideway Transit and Passenger Rail Systems. It is a standard for the US for the design of rail systems, and it focuses on the safety and fire related aspects of station and rail tunnel design. Produced by the National Fire Protection Association in the US, it contains many proscriptive requirements for the design of underground stations. This standard is used and followed extensively in the US and Asia, but not in Europe, where European Union and national standards are used.

NFPA 130 discusses a number of topics, and this includes chapter 2 on the design of underground stations. In this chapter are some requirements on materials for underground stations, fire protection of staff and other areas, but also three requirements that are used extensively in station design. These are:
- Platforms must be able to be evacuated in 4 minutes or less (but not necessarily out of the station)
- The entire station should be capable of being evacuated in 6 minutes or less
- The maximum distance from any point on a platform to an exit should be no greater than 300 feet (or 91.4 metres)

The standard also provides for estimating the number of people that should be used for any simulation of the escape time from the station. This is based on the capacity of trains entering the station for each platform, and the number of people that might be waiting to board a train, multiplied by a safety factor, commonly 2. The modelling of the design of the station then involves estimating how long the station takes to evacuate, and a compliant design can evacuate passengers in less than the required time.

The use of NFPA 130 seems to be popular in Asia and Australia, and is obviously common in North America. It is also used in South America. It is not mandatory in Asia or Australia at all, and has no legal force, but seems to be popular because of its clear and easy to understand rules on what is acceptable or not. In Australia the standard is often used as a reference without being strictly applied. Commonly a station that is designed to NFPA 130 will have a number of easy to reach exits, which are quite wide that can accommodate large numbers of people. A long platform such as 300 metres long will have at least 4 exits, and each will be designed to allow a lot of people to pass through.

NFPA 130 also contains the provision that the entire station must be evacuated in 6 minutes or less. This means that there needs to be enough room for people to move quickly from the paid to the unpaid area. Turnstiles and barriers are common in most stations, to stop fare evaders from entering the paid area without a ticket, but in times of emergency they can impede the flow of passengers from the station. Consider that a metro station will typically have at least 2 platforms, and each metro train can typically take up to 3000 people, so a design load of 9000 people for an emergency is not unreasonable. They will need to be able to exit the station quickly, and through barriers and turnstiles. NFPA provides that a typical number for the people per minute that can move through a turnstile is 25, so that means a large metro station will require at least 60 turnstiles. That's an extremely large number, and unlikely to be implemented in practice, so another solution is necessary.

In some rail systems there are alternative exits and staircases available for passengers in the event of a fire. These hidden staircases are opened when a fire emergency starts, and there is a need to evacuate the station. As most metro stations are very busy, and have large numbers of passengers, it is not surprising that in an emergency it is not possible to evacuate the station in the time required under NFPA130. A solution to this is to provide another entirely separate set of staircases, much like fire escapes in large buildings, but with some differences. These exits are controlled by the fire alarm system, and are not accessible unless there is some sort of emergency. They also have no barriers, or turnstiles, as this would slow the movement of passengers out of the station. Another interesting feature of these "secret" exits is that they only need to connect the platform to a place where passengers can exit safely, and this may include another part of the station. Typically these exits connect the platform area to the concourse of a station, but outside of the paid area, so that passenger escape is not limited by difficult to move through barriers.

Research has found that people fleeing a fire will not attempt to escape through an exit that is obscured by smoke. This is even the case where that exit is the only safe way to escape a fire. For this reason a major focus of any underground station design is to ensure that any exit indentified for escape from a fire should be ventilated sufficiently that smoke cannot accumulate there to appear to block the exit. This often means that there should be large air-conditioning ducts located close to the exit to clear any smoke, and this needs to be considered when constructing the station.

The cost of management and construction of an underground station is much higher than for above ground stations. Above ground stations have a much lower risk profile, and this translates into lower operating and maintenance costs. Underground stations require complex fire protection and ventilation systems, which make them much more expensive to build, and need to be monitored. Complex ventilation systems need to be maintained, and the need to be supervised in a control centre somewhere. Again, this all adds costs.

Modelling of smoke flow in a station is very important, as this allows analysis of the safe places in the station, the correct means of escape, and how large a fire needs to be before there are fatalities. These types of models are commonly reported on in journals and conference papers, and may be three dimensional models of stations where smoke moves outwards from a large fire. In the models fires are almost always placed in trains stopped at the stations, and small to large fires are modelled. The amount of smoke evolved from a fire of different sizes is estimated, and then the smoke allowed to flow through the station to see what happens.

Particularly complex models can allow for the movement of passengers through the station, moving away from the smoke. The intention is that passengers can escape the fire without too much difficulty. It should be noted that a very large fire is difficult for passengers to escape from, and even the best designed underground station will have difficulty in protecting passengers. The types of things that the modelling is looking for is:

- Can small fires cause fatalities?
- Will the design of the station cause people to be trapped if the fire is in specific unlucky locations?
- Are slow moving passengers unable to escape even small fires?
- Does smoke moves in an unpredictable way, and traps people in an unexpected part of the station?
- If the station is safe during non-peak times, is it more dangerous during peak times when the passenger load is larger?

Should fire and life safety modelling of a station reveal any of these problems then the station will need to be redesigned. The redesign will then need to be modelled to ensure that any detected problems have been removed.

Infrastructure in an Underground Station

With many of the engineering systems installed into rail tunnels, they are installed into rooms where this equipment sits and performs its function when the rail tunnel is operating. These needs to be placed at stations and strategic locations through the rail tunnel, and a location needs to be found for them. The short list of rooms and plant are:

- A control room
- Ventilation rooms
- Fire control rooms
- Water treatment plant
- Substations (power rooms)
- Communications rooms
- Water pumping stations

Maintainers will need access to these rooms, as will emergency services and police in the event of any emergency. The number and size of these can have a powerful effect on the cost of a rail tunnel.

Along with the ducts and pumps come flow meters, pressure gauges, and temperature sensors. These are quite useful, and are used to monitor the flow of air. These meters and gauges are connected to the control room, so the control room operator can see what air is moving, and where to, and what temperature it is. Air conditioning systems in underground tunnels usually work quite well, and provide very few problems.

All the ventilation equipment is normally contained within a room, often located in underground stations. These rooms are sometimes called ventilation rooms. Depending on the design of the tunnel, the need for fresh air, etc, one or two ventilation rooms are needed in each location. As with any infrastructure, keeping the amount needed to a minimum is the key to efficient construction and maintenance.

Tunnels can also have a control room, where operators are assigned to monitor the tunnel. This is a pretty boring job, as very little happens and operators are there for emergencies. The control room has visibility over the different engineering systems, what is happening, and the movement of trains. Control rooms for tunnels DO NOT control the movement of trains, but they can see where the trains are. The function of controlling the movement of trains may be near by, or even located in the same room, but the function is different to managing a rail tunnel. The role of the computer system that oversees the control room is a little controversial, as some favour a high level of involvement for any automatic system, and others prefer the operators to make decisions on what should happen in the event of an emergency.

A control room is a place where a number of operators sit and watch screens all day. Often very dark, operators seem to like to sit in relative darkness to watch screens. The control room is connected to all the various different systems, and if a problem occurs on any of them, then the computer system generates an alarm. An alarm is both an audible alarm, as well as something on the screen designed to catch the eye of the operator. If a fire starts in the tunnel, then alarms will start ringing from the control panel.

From day to day very little happens in tunnels, and incidents are rare (or should be rare). One control room can monitor hundreds of kilometres of tunnel before they require a second person. A very wasteful and inefficient thing to do is create a short tunnel that requires a control room, with very little to do, because a control room is expensive, and it's bad practise to create one for a short rail tunnel. Its best, where there are several rail tunnels in close proximity to one another, to combine all the control rooms into a single room which monitors them all.

Many rail tunnels provide something called "escape". It is considered desirable in many countries that if there is an emergency in a tunnel, then passengers have a reasonable chance to flee the area, and escape should be provided. Escape usually means walkways down the side of the rail tunnel, which increases the size of the tunnel, and hence it's cost. Escape is also the reason why twin bore rail tunnels are used instead of single bore, as passengers can escape down one of the tunnels and leave the tunnel with the emergency in it. Having twin bore tunnels is extremely expensive, and should be done only when there is a clear need to do so.

A communications room is the place where all the information on what is happening in the tunnel is relayed back to the control room, and potentially other locations where the tunnel is monitored. The local fire brigade may be given some monitoring over the tunnel, especially if the tunnel is in a metropolitan area. Also security companies may monitor doors and access to the tunnel, and respond where someone has accessed the facility and not been authorised to do so. Communications rooms are full of banks of modems, switches, power supplies and cabling.

The fire control room is a room where the fire brigade, or similar organisation, can attend a fire emergency, and control the various systems in both underground tunnels and stations. The fire control room is located in a place where large vehicles can be parked, and where access is easy. The fire control room provides control over lifts and escalators, lighting, water and hydrants, as well as power. There may be many fire control rooms, for example, one at each station, and at any tunnel portals. That can be a large number.

A substation is a place where the power is provided to the station and tunnels. Incoming power is normally the wrong voltage for use in a station, so it needs to be converted to a more useful voltage. This room is sometimes called the power room. Inside the substation are transformers and busbars that allow power to be distributed to the different pieces of equipment that require power. The placement of a substation can be very important, because occasionally substations catch fire, and so this risk needs to be managed. As substations are potential sources of fire, they would never be placed in the middle of an island platform surrounded by passengers, unless there was simply no other option.

Tunnels

Many rail lines include some tunnels. Tunnelling is often needed to complete rail lines when it is geographically difficult for trains to move above ground. Commonly, in cities rail lines are of tunnelled, so that houses and buildings on the surface do not need to be demolished. Tunnelling is often seen as being a sensible and safe way of moving trains from one place to another.

Tunnels have many specialist engineering systems that are not installed anyway else in a rail system. Naturally for any rail tunnel there will be a signalling system, track and rails, drainage, and a power system, but these are common to all rail systems regardless of whether they are in a tunnel or not.

Rail tunnels are an underground passage where trains can pass through. They can be constructed through a variety of different methods, and the choice of method can strongly influence the cost of the tunnelling. There is often no alternative but to tunnel a rail line, and so the rail line becomes very expensive to build. It is important to note that tunnelling should be avoided if at all possible in any new rail line. It is undesirable for any rail line to be tunnelled, and it's only done where there is no alternative. The reader may assume that as the world is filling up with rail tunnels that tunnelling is desirable, it's not, and should only be used as a last resort when there is simply no alternative. Unfortunately, frequently there is no alternative.

Tunnels are often used when:
- Rail lines need to pass through cities and there is a desire not to demolish buildings

- Rail lines need to pass through an area with mountains or hills, and it is impractical to go around of over the hills or mountains
- Rail lines need to move from one land mass to another, with a body of water in between, and it is impractical to build a bridge over the water

Possibly one of the most famous rail tunnels is the Chunnel, the rail line that links Great Britain with continental Europe. This is one of the longest rail tunnels in the world although far from the longest. The longest rail tunnel at the time of writing of this book is the Gothard Base tunnel in Switzerland, which is 57 kms long.

Despite the popularity of tunnelling, it is actually very expensive. As a rough guide (in 2012 US dollars), a tunnelled metro line costs approx. $100 million US per kilometre to build, which is approx. five times more than the comparable cost for construction above ground. This is just an indicative figure, and tunnels can cost far more than this, and depending on how they are built, the costs can exceed $200 million per route kilometre. This is especially so where there are multiple separate tunnels running next to each other, and underground emergency stations constructed with no access to the surface. Rail tunnels also are expensive to maintain, costing up to $3 US million per year per track kilometre.

The most important variable for a rail tunnel is its length. Longer tunnels require more safety equipment, and are generally much more expensive to construct even on a per metre basis. As tunnels get longer the problems with them generally become more serious. A common length for a tunnel, when many more asset items are required, is about 1 kilometre. Very short tunnels, such as 200 or 300 metres, rarely present many problems. Tunnels over 5 kilometres require all sorts of specialist equipment.

Tunnels can be used by either freight, passengers, or for both. Freight tunnels are probably rarer than passenger tunnels, but may be common the US. Freight moving through tunnels can be problematic, as most freight is diesel powered, and this means exhaust fumes. Tunnels are a confined space, these fumes accumulate, and can present a real risk to any staff on the train. The smaller the tunnel, the greater this problem. Obviously this problem can be addressed with lots of ventilation, but rail freight is usually built with very limited budgets, and the money is often not available to build the tunnel and a complicated ventilation system.

So the question the reader may be asking is: why is tunnel design so problematic? What's the issue? Why not simply install the best possible systems and safety and so everyone can enjoy the benefits of improved security and safety in rail tunnels. Surely building the best possible tunnel is the correct decision?

The problem is that each additional system installed into a tunnel costs a lot of money, and the improvement in safety is very small. As more engineering systems are installed, the cost per kilometre increases. Each additional system assists with the management of fires in tunnels, but none of these systems actually put the fire out. As they don't put the fire out, there is always another one to install, and each reduces the risk a little further. The graph below attempts to demonstrate the problem:

Construction Cost vs Safety Risk

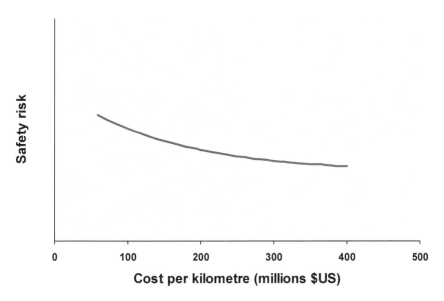

As the cost of the tunnel increases, then the cost per kilometre also increases. Unfortunately, the number of systems that can be installed in a tunnel is now very great, and even more are being invented. This creates the situation where no one railway could possibly install all of the systems, at best most could be installed, but even that would be prohibitively expensive. A compromise is needed, and a decision for each new rail line is needed as to what to install and what level of safety to accept.

At this stage we should note that the fire risk in almost any rail tunnel is low. Whilst much of the design of rail tunnels concerns fire safety, the risk of an incident occurring in any one tunnel is extremely small. In many cases a rail system designer could simply ignore the risk, and operate without any of the mitigations to safety that are common to manage fire risk, and nothing would happen. Fire systems in rail tunnels are installed to protect against very rare events. Where additional safety systems are installed, the reduction in risk can be very small, so much so that it can be difficult to justify the additional cost of the extra safety system.

This is why the engineering standards are so important. They represent a compromise where transport system designers and engineers can say that enough in terms of safety has been done. The choice of number and type of systems to install in a rail tunnel can become very contentious, as safety is often a controversial topic. When a tunnel meets a specific standard, then this provides an explanation as to how the tunnel was designed and safety decisions made. Designing a rail tunnel to a well-defined standard is one way of managing the safety risk.

The alternative to using a standard is to perform a risk analysis and apply the ALARP principle. ALARP stands for As Low As Reasonably Practical, and it's a commonly used principle in safety science. In practice it's hard to apply, and generating a worthwhile usable assessment of tunnel safety is not easy, but it can be done. One of the problems is assessing how frequently accidents would occur with different safety systems installed. This estimate is difficult to generate as accidents in tunnels are very rare, and so useful statistics are challenging to get. Another problem is that a determination is needed on the value of a human life, and this needs to be included in the equation. Any calculation that places a value on a human life is always controversial. For these reasons it is often preferred to design a rail standard with reference to standards and other official documents.

If the country in which the tunnel is being constructed has standards or regulations, then things are easy. The European Union has issued a directive on what tunnel systems to design, and this is very helpful. Many European countries, in addition to the EU directives, have standards or laws that directly proscribe how tunnels should be designed. The US has a tunnel design standard, so this provides a high level of information and detail on how to design a rail tunnel.

The European Union directive 2008/163/EC, and the US standard represent two quite different ways of designing rail tunnels. In addition to the many national standards that exist, and Switzerland, Austria and Germany all have their own standards on what is acceptable and what is not in a tunnel. Almost nothing is common between both of the standards, which is unfortunate.

So what systems are we talking about here? Extra systems installed in tunnels include:

- Control room for tunnel systems
- Radio rebroadcast system
- Communications backbone
- Cross passages (this is between double bore tunnels only)
- HVAC systems
- Lighting
- Mobile phone system
- Security systems
- Fire detection
- Hydrants and provision of water to fire fighting services
- Telephone systems (which are different to the mobile phone system)
- Water treatment

That's a lot of systems, and almost all of these are required only for rail tunnels. Older rail tunnels did not have this amount, and were built just as holes in the ground with a train moving through it. Many of the older tunnels have not been upgraded, because the cost of doing this is high, and so they have been left largely as they were first designed and constructed. New tunnels are technically more complex, and rail tunnelling projects are more complex than what they were 50 years ago.

In additional to the engineering systems listed above, there are a number of features of rail tunnels that are also relevant to the cost and difficulty of building the tunnel. Not all of these features of the tunnel are an engineering system, but rather something that is added to the tunnel, and makes it more expensive to build. For example walkways, which run alongside the tunnel, allow people to alight from the train in an emergency. It's not strictly speaking a system, but a flat space where people can walk. Some of these additional features are:

- Twin bore tunnel system, which is composed of two tunnels instead of one. Constructing two tunnels increases the cost of the tunnel dramatically, and should be done only when absolutely necessary
- Twin tunnels, and a third access tunnel. This means three tunnels need to be dug, and the cost for kilometre will be extremely high

- Escape walkways, which run alongside the tunnel, allowing passengers the opportunity to walk along and escape for any potential fire. Escape walkways are especially expensive for twin bore tunnels, as they significantly increase the size of the tunnel, and hence it's construction cost
- Pressure relief vents, which reduce the pressure of air in front of a HSR train.
- A full underground station, which has no connection with the surface, which is used only for very long tunnels and for letting passengers move from one tube in a twin tunnel system to another.

The cheapest per linear metre tunnel is a short one where none of the above systems or features are needed. For longer tunnels more and more is needed, and for genuinely long tunnels almost all the systems listed above would be installed. For a short tunnel of 100 metres, almost none of the systems would be installed.

Identified is some of the commonality of designs for rail tunnels, and what seems to be the consensus for rail tunnels. The author has attempted to put together a guide for what is required for tunnels of different length. Obviously, it is necessary to be quite broad, as the reference materials/standards themselves are vague or don't agree. The table below is really just a rough guide.

Tunnels and the Systems/Features Installed		
Tunnel length		**Typical systems installed**
Very short	<300 metres	Tunnel lighting only, no ventilation nor escape walkways provided. A bare tunnel, almost always single bore.
Short	300 – 1000 metres	May or may not have ventilation, or escape or any other system, depending on which standard and regulation was applied. There's no real guidance for what to do with tunnels of this length
Medium	1000 – 3000 metres	Usually single bore, but with many of the safety systems installed, including hydrants, escape

Tunnels and the Systems/Features Installed

Tunnel length		Typical systems installed
		walkways, communications, and ventilation. Potentially some of this is not needed if the tunnel is particularly large or no freight passes through the tunnel.
Long	3000 – 15,000 metres	These tunnels may or may not be double bore, but will have complex ventilation systems, communication systems, and monitoring.
Very long	>15,000 metres	This tunnel will have every system available installed, including double bore tunnels with potentially a third access tunnel, and underground escape stations. Ventilation systems will be very sophisticated, and a dedicated control room will be required. Very expensive to build and maintain

So the key to success for any rail tunnel is to keep the length as short as possible. A good way to reduce the cost of any new rail line is to split long tunnels into many smaller ones, and both the European and US standards/directives explicitly acknowledge that this can be an effective strategy. The EU directive provides that 500 metres between successive tunnels is enough to break them up, from one large tunnel, into two smaller ones.

Ventilation in Tunnels

There is a commonly held view that almost any fire emergency can be managed with ventilation. The idea is that when a fire occurs in a rail tunnel, the operator in the control room can push a few buttons, and passengers can make their way to safety. Ventilation can be used to eliminate the smoke and provide a clear escape path from the train to safety. This is considered to be the case even in single bore tunnels.

Single bore tunnels have no alternative for passengers to go in an emergency except forwards or backwards. In a double bore tunnel passengers can move from one tunnel to another, and in this situation ventilation can be useful to prevent smoke from getting from the tunnel with the fire to the tunnel without the fire. Double bore tunnels require ventilation to ensure one of the tunnels is free of smoke

However for single bore tunnels ventilation semingly has limited benefits. The author is very suspicious of any assertion that fires can be managed with ventilation. Fires require oxygen to continue burning, and ventilating a fire is an excellent way to dramatically increase the size and smoke evolved in a fire. Fires can often be suppressed by removing their oxygen supply, and adding air to a fire is a genuinely bad idea.

Also, consider that during a fire emergency in a single bore tunnel, passengers will alight from the train and head towards one end of the tunnel or another. Passengers on either side of the fire will move away from the fire, and so passengers will flee in opposite directions. Any control room operator that actives a ventilation system needs to send the smoke in one direction or another, and for anyone that has the smoke blown towards them, it's almost certain death. There is little point in having a safety system that only kills half the people in an emergency.

Also consider the poor control room operator, there are almost never cameras in tunnels, as the tunnel is dark and there is nothing to see. So the decision on which direction to send the ventilation is an impossible one, as there is almost no information on where the passengers are, and where the fire is burning. There are so many things that can go wrong.

Even in double bore tunnels, ventilation has serious limitations on how it can assist with a fire emergency. It's best with double bore tunnels there are no open connections between the two tunnels, but sometimes crossovers are installed, or a terminating road, or some other stabling underground, in which case the smoke can move easily from one tunnel to another. Smoke can travel 2 kms in a large fire, and so the two tunnels really need to be properly separated from each. The same can be said for underground stations, where the smoke can move from one tunnel to another. The priority in a station, in a fire emergency, is to keep emergency exits free of smoke, and there may not be the equipment to stop the fire moving from one tunnel to another.

Given that large volumes of smoke can be emitted in a fire emergency, and that smoke moves quite quickly, the benefits of twin bore tunnels is lost where there are frequent stations, or large open sections between the two tunnels, such as for a cross or terminating road. This is the reason why the use of double bore tunnels is normally limited to long rail tunnels with very few or no stations at all.

Ventilation in single bore tunnels allows fire fighting authorities to fight fires in tunnels. The smoke emitted from a fire can be very great, and without proper ventilation it may be difficult to access any burning material. Ventilation will allow the smoke to be managed, and push it to a place out of the way of firefighters, allowing the fire to be brought under control. Fires that burn for long periods can substantially damage the walls of a tunnel, and it is important to ensure that this does not happen. For any reasonable size tunnel, some form of ventilation should be provided, to allow the tunnel to be protected in the event of a fire emergency.

Groundwater in Tunnels

One of the many challenges in managing tunnels is removing the groundwater that seeps through the walls and into the tunnel. In most places the ground is full of water, and when a tunnel is dug through then the water moves into the tunnel. This water is full of minerals, and can have a very dirty appearance. Iron oxide is a common contaminant of this water, and gives the water a dark brown appearance. Groundwater is often located in aquifers, which is basically porous rock. Once a tunnel is dug through an aquifer, then the water in it starts emptying into the tunnel. In some cases this can be a lot of water.

The treatment of groundwater is an interesting problem, and the temptation is to pump it directly into the sea or nearby body in water. In practice groundwater recovered from rail tunnels will be cleaned and then used for whatever purpose water is needed in the nearby area. This will sometimes be for irrigation, or possibly for drinking. Often the water is just pumped into a river after some basic processing and cleaning.

Groundwater seeps into the tunnel through the walls, and the quality of the wall material determines the amount of water that seeps through. The water drips down the walls, and then collects at the bottom of the tunnel. Tunnels are normally designed so that this water can be collected and processed, and then sent to where ever its final destination is. Over very long tunnels the volume of water can be quite large, and hundreds of thousand of litres of water per day is not uncommon.

The flow of water into a tunnel is normally measured in litres per kilometre per second. For example, a common measure is 0.5 litres per kilometre per second, which over a long tunnel can become a lot of water. This number changes depending on the ground conditions, and the quantity of water in the ground.

Where the waterproofing of a tunnel is poor, the tunnel will be wet and covered with slime. This type of tunnel is quite messy and disgusting to go into, as there is water everywhere. Whilst almost all passengers do not see or care what condition a tunnel is in, it is better for engineering management if a tunnel is not in this kind of condition, as the water gets into the signalling and electrical equipment, and replacement programs are needed to keep the equipment functioning. There is a tradeoff between construction cost and the waterproofing of the tunnel walls, with better waterproofing leading to less water ingress.

Groundwater is not dangerous to humans, normally it is safe to drink, but it's a bit disgusting, so many people won't drink it. There are towns in the US and Canada where the water quality is so poor that tunnel water obtained from almost any tunnel in Australia is cleaner that what some towns are drinking. One has some sympathy for these poor people.

Where a rail tunnel passes either under a river, or is below sea water, then the amount of water ingress can be quite large. Tunnels typically drain all the water from the nearby rock over a period of years, so the water ingress will slowly reduce. Tunnels located below rivers or below sea level will always have a high level of water ingress, and this water needs to be managed. The nearby river bed with put the water back into the ground that has drained into the tunnel, water ingress into the tunnel will continue as long as there is water flowing in the river. Obviously most seas won't disappear, and oceans are very unlikely to disappear, although the Aral Sea in Russia has almost disappeared, but this is rare.

One of the many challenges with water entering a tunnel is that a rail tunnel can drain the nearby land of most of its water. This can lead to the ground subsiding, or sinking, and where this problem is particularly bad, the ground can collapse into the rail tunnel. In Sydney during the construction of a road tunnel around 2009, this problem led to the destruction of an entire block of flats, which collapsed into the hole left by the ground subsiding. Fortunately no one was hurt, but it makes for good television, and is very poor publicity for the construction company building the infrastructure. Where rail tunnels are built in populated areas, which seemingly is most of the time, then the condition of the tunnel walls will need to be good to prevent houses being damaged above the excavated tunnels. Rail system designers should note that tunnels through parks, or areas in cities where there are no structures, may be cheaper because the preparation of the walls of the tunnel can be less costly and more simple.

So the big question for any rail tunnel is: what to do with the water? A long rail tunnel will generate a lot of water, and where can it go? Stormwater drains are usually for water from streets and other runoff, and it may or may not be possible to put the water there. Sewerage systems are normally for human waste, and have limited capacity, so the local sewerage company may not accept the water either. Pumping the water into a nearby stream or creek may disturb the wildlife there, or potentially kill it. It's not easy to get rid of so much water.

So the things that can be done to dispose of the water include:
- Use it for irrigation, toilets, washing hard surfaces and other requirements that need only low quality water
- Process it and pump it into a river, lake, or other body of water
- Process it so that it is clean and drinkable, and sell it back to the local water provider
- Clean it and then use it for drinking water in nearby stations, ie, shops in the station
- Power stations needs water, so a nearby power station will pay for a source of water
- Some industrial facilities or factories need water, so it can be pumped to them

Most of the strategies above involve some level of processing water. To do this a facility is needed called a water treatment plant, which is capable of taking waste water and processing it into cleaner (or less dirty) water. The cleaner the water at the end of the process, the more expensive the water treatment plant. Normally it's best if a rail line has only one water treatment plant, as they cost millions of dollars, so that means there is a system of pipes running from the tunnel to the plant. These pipes run everywhere, so things do get a bit complicated. Water treatment plants often use chemicals to clean the water, so these needs to be stored, and provision made if they leak, etc. Also some space needs to be found for the plant, as water treatment plants can be quite large.

Tunnels in Remote Areas

Rail tunnels are often located in remote places. Tunnels allow rail lines to move through difficult geography, or through mountains. Typically major cities are built on plains, or near the ocean or sea, and not on mountains, so rail lines that pass through mountains are often far from cities.

As discussed above, for a long tunnel, a number of equipment rooms are needed, such as communications rooms, power rooms, ventilation and water pumping stations. This is a lot of equipment, and requires power and communications to operate. For many of the tunnels in remote areas, this can pose a significant problem.

In Australia large forests still exist and rail lines with long tunnels pass through them. Many of these tunnels are quite long, 1 to 3 kilometres, and so based on what was said above, really should need lots of engineering systems. This however presents a problem, because these systems need lots of power and communications. Where rail tunnels are located in large forests or in mountain ranges, providing power to remote locations is not easy, and is fraught with many challenges. Access roads will need to be cut, power cables or transmission lines are needed to the tunnel, and areas are needed for equipment to be stored and vehicles are parked.

Whilst the EU directive and the US NFPA130 does not allow for any change in equipment provided in a tunnel based on its location, in practice tunnels in remote locations often have very little equipment, at least in Australia. The cost to maintain, and for staff to reach the tunnel, makes installing anything more than lighting and basic communications economically impossible. This is especially so in large national parks, where environmental departments strongly dislike rail maintainers cutting access roads through 40 million year old rain forest.

Where a tunnel is located in pristine rainforest, no one likes cutting large access roads through the forest. The reality is there is often some endangered species living somewhere near the road, and if the access road is created, some of these species will be killed. It's almost unavoidable, and when this happens other government departments other than the railway may get very upset. Overall it's best not to put access roads through environmentally sensitive areas, but where a large tunnel is installed, then an access road is needed for maintenance staff to go there and check equipment, perform inspections, and do minor maintenance.

The author suggests that in this situation, a "consenting adults" approach is needed to any equipment installed in rail tunnels in remote or environmentally sensitive areas. For rail tunnels under 3 kilometres in length, where it is located in a area difficult to access, it may be acceptable to not install all the equipment that would normally go with that tunnel. Very large tunnels, or with lots of passenger traffic, will still need all of the systems described above, but for thinly used rail lines, maybe it's not needed. Certainly in Australia in these remote tunnels there is nothing installed at all, in many cases not even lighting. Obviously it is possible to install less equipment, but what, and when? All of this raises many questions.

Building a rail tunnel in a remote environment, or in an environmentally sensitive area can create problems. The installation of equipment, in a tunnel in a remote environment, may create substantial problems, and it may be best to either lengthen the tunnel so that access through a sensitive area is not needed and the tunnel systems can be installed more easily, or shorten it so that any tunnel systems are not needed. A longer tunnel, which starts from a more accessible location, can be a good way to resolve the issues that occur when building a tunnel in a sensitive area.

HSR Tunnels

Many problems exist when building and designing tunnels for highs speed rail services. High speed trains entering rail tunnels can experience what many people describe as a "sonic boom", which can be quite unsettling to passengers and particularly those living around the rail line. Another problem that can occur with particularly long tunnels is a drop in air pressure as the train makes its way along the tunnel. As the air pressure drops, passengers can feel nauseated, and may feel sick. One solution to this problem is to slow the trains down, or seal or at least partially seal the high speed train such that passengers do not feel the drop in pressure.

Again, as with safety systems for tunnels, minimising the length of a rail tunnel can be an effective way of reducing problems with air pressure in tunnels. As an HSR train progresses through a rail tunnel, the problems with pressure get worse as the train moves through the tunnel, and the longer inside the tunnel, the worse the problems get. HSR trains are often partially sealed, so external pressure differences will only effect passengers if the train is in the tunnel for a long time. The better the seal, the slower the pressure in the train will reduce. Regardless of the quality of the sealing of the train, in a very long tunnel even the best train will experience a large drop in pressure, which will be uncomfortable for passengers.

REFERENCES

1. Zhang, C. & Li, L. Zhang, D. & Zhang, S. *Types and Characteristics of Safety Accidents Induced by Metro Construction*, 2009 International Conference on Information Management, Innovation Management and Industrial Engineering, 209

2. Chief Fire and Rescue Advisor *GRA 4.2 Incidents involving transport systems - rail*, Communities and Local Government Fire and Rescue Service Operational Guide, 2011

3. Parsons Brinkerhoff *High Speed Rail*, Network, Issue No 73, Sept 2011, http://www.pbworld.com/news/publications.aspx

4. gruner, Aerodynamics, Ventilation and Tunnel Safety for High Speed Rail Tunnels, paginas.fe.up.pt/~hsrt/documents/RudolfBopp_abs_001.pdf, Oct 2009

5. Chow, W.K. *Ventilation of enclosed train compartments in Hong Kong*, Applied Energy 71 (2002) 161-170

6. NFPA130 2000, *Standard for Fixed Guideway Transit and Passenger Rail Systems*, 2000 Edition

7. Rail Accident Investigation Branch *Technical Investigation Report concerning the Fire on Eurotunnel Freight Shuttle 7412 on September 2008*, November 2010 (in French)

8. Illinois Department of Health Commonly Found Substances in Drinking Water and Available Treatment, http://www.idph.state.il.us/envhealth/pdf/DrinkingWater.pdf

9. Agriculture and Resource Management Council of Australia and New Zealand & Australia and New Zealand Environment and Conversation Council *Guidelines for Sewerage Systems Acceptance of Trade Waste (Industrial Waste)*, November 1994

10. Krasyuk, A. *Calculation of Tunnel Ventilation in Shallow Subways*, Journal of Mining Science, Vol 41, No 3, 2005

11. Efron N, & Read, N *Analysing International Tunnel Costs*, Worcester Polytechnic Institute, Feb 2012

12. ARUP Burnley Tunnel Fire – The ARUP View, April 2007, http://www.index-files.com/file-pdf/burnley-tunnel-fire-the-arup-view-tunnel-details

13. Zuber, P. *Compared Safety Features for Rail Tunnels* First International Symposium, Prague 2004, Safe and Reliable Tunnels. Innovation European Achievements

14. Woods, E. *Bored Tunnels,* The Arup Journal, 1/2004

15. Twine, D. *Cut-and-Cover Tunnels* The Arup Journal, 1/2004

16. Tarada, F. *Critical Velocities for Smoke Control in Tunnel Cross-Passages*, First International Conference on Major Tunnel and Infrastructure Projects, May 2000, Taiwan

17. Smith, G. & Ceranic, B. *Spatial Layout Planning in Sub-Surface Rail Station Design for Effective Fire Evacuation*, Architectural Engineering and Design Management, 2008, Volume 4, Pages 99 – 120

18. Ghiasi, V. et al *Design Criteria of Subway Tunnels* Australian Journal of Basic and Applied Sciences, 4(12): 5894-5907, 2010

19. European Parliament *Assessment of the Safety of Tunnels Study*, (IP/A/STOA/FWC/2005-28/SC22/29)

20. Ghiasi, V. et al *Construction Regulations along Metro Alignment*, Australian Journal of Basic and Applied Sciences, 4(12): 5972-6009, 2010

21. Federal Department of the Environment, Transport, Energy, Directive: *Roads tunnels doors and gates*, Astra, 13 011, Swiss confederation

22. GHD Pty Ltd, *The Design of the Lane Cove River Cut and Cover Tunnels and Cofferdam for the Epping to Chatswood Rail Line*, ASEC Conference, 2005

23. European Union, *Directive 2001/16/EC/ - Draft Technical Specification for Interoperability: Aspect Safety in Rail Tunnels*

24. Thamm, B. *The new EU Directive on Road and Tunnel Safety*, International Symposium on Tunnel Safety and Security, November 2004

25.Bopp, R & Hagennah, B. Aerodynamics, Ventilation and Tunnel Safety for High Speed Rail Tunnels, http://paginas.fe.up.pt/~hsrt/documents/RudolfBopp_abs_001.pdf

26. Miclea, P. et al *International Tunnel Fire-Safety Design Practices*, Ashrae Journal, Aug 2007

27. Queensland Co-ordinator General Northern Link Road Tunnel, April 2010, http://www.statedevelopment.qld.gov.au/resources/project/legacy-way-project/northern-link-road-tunnel-cg-report.pdf

28. Varol, A. & Dalgic, S. *Grouting Applications in the Instanbul Metro, Turkey*, Tunnelling and Underground Space Technology 21 (2006) 602-612

29. Reinke, R. & Ravn, S. Twin-Tube, *Single-Track High Speed Rail Tunnels and Consequences for Aerodynamics*, Climate, Equipment and Ventilation, 2004 International Conference on Tunnelling, Asia, New Dehli

30. N'Kaoua et al *A parametric study into the factors affecting the development and alleviation of micro-pressure waves in railway tunnels*, BHR Group

31. Xiang, X. & Lei-Ping, X. *Tunnel hood effects on high speed train-tunnel compression wave*, 9th International Conference on Hydrodynamics, 2010 Shanghai, China

32. Klinger, R. *Radio Coverage for Road and Rail Tunnels in Tunnels in the Frequency Range 75 to 1000 MHz*, Vehicular Technology Conference, 1991.

33. Hewitt, P. *Groundwater Control for Sydney Rock Tunnels*, AGS AUCTA Mini-Symposium: Geotechnical Aspects of Tunneling for Infrastructure Projects, Oct 2005

34. Quqing, G. *Metro Tunnelling in China*, Tunnelling and Underground Space Technology, Vol 5, No 3, pp 271 – 275, 1990

35. Gabay, D. *Compared Fire Safety Features for Metro Tunnels*, Safe and Reliable Tunnels, First International Symposium, Prague 2004

36. Soons, C.J. et al *Framework of a quantitative risk analysis fore the fire safety in metro systems*, Tunnelling and Underground Space Technology 21 (2006) 281

37. Beard, A. *Tunnel safety, risk assessment and decision-making*, Tunnelling and Underground Space Technology, 25 (2010) 91 – 94

38. Muller, M. Tunnel Safety; where we are now, http://www.imia.com/wp-content/uploads/2013/05/EP22-2005-Tunnel-Safety-Where-are-we-now.pdf

39. OECD Norway Tunnel Safety, 2006, http://www.oecd.org/norway/36100776.pdf

40. Yoon SW, & Choi, H. *Development of Quantitative Risk Analysis Tool for the Fire Safety in Railway Tunnel*, International Forum on Decision Making, Japan May 2009

41. Liu, Tang-hong. *Design and Optimisation of tunnel hoods*, Tunnelling Underground Space Technology 25 (2010) 212-219

42. Williams, R. & Chalmers, G. *Recent Developments in the Design of Cut and Cover Construction for Railway Tunnels and Stations*, Conference on Railway Engineering, Adelaide, May 2000

43. Krenn, F. et al *Shallow Tunnelling in Soft Ground – Influence of the Chosen Support System on the System Behaviour*, Geomechanik und Tunnelbau 1 (2008), Heft 3

44. Kim, Y. & Bruland, A. *Effect of rock mass quality on construction time in a road tunnel*, Tunnelling and Underground Space Technology 24 (2009) 584-591

45. Cheong, SW. *Fire Safety Design for Rapid Transit Systems*, Proceedings of the international conference, Fire India, 2004

46. Tarada, F. & King, M. *Structural Fire Protection of Railway Tunnels*, Railway Engineering Conference, University of Westminster, UK, June 2009

47. Wagner, H. *The Governance of Cost in Tunnel Design and Construction*, 1 Congresso Brasilero de Tuneis e Estruturas Subterraneas Seminario Internacional South American Tunnelling

48. Neumann, C. et al Koralm Tunnel – Development of Tunnel System Design and Safety Concept, http://www.ilf.com/fileadmin/user_upload/publikationen/39_Koralm_T unnel_Development_of_Tunnel_System_Design_and_Safety_Concept. pdf

49. United Nations Inland Transport Committee *Recommendations of the Multi-Disciplinary Group of Experts on Safety in Tunnels (Rail)*, TRANS/AC.9/9 Dec 2003

50. International Technology Scanning Program *Underground Transportation Systems in Europe: Safety, Operations, and Emergency Response*, FHWA-PL-06-016, June 2006

51. BHBB Cross City Tunnel Joint Venture *Construction Compliance Report for the Cross City Tunnel Project*, http://www.crosscity.com.au/files/documents/15_1st-environment-report-jan-july03.pdf

52. Haack, A. *Water Leakages in Subsurface Facilities: Required Watertightness, Contractual Methods and Methods of Redevelopment*, Journal of Tunnelling and Underground Space Technology, Vol 6, Number 3, pp 273 – 282, 1991

53. Yuan, Y. et al *Tunnel Waterproofing Practices in China*, Tunnelling and Underground Space Technology, Vol 15, No 2, pp 227 – 233, 2000

54. *The Handbook of Tunnel Fire Safety*, edited by Alan Beard and Richard Carvel, 2005

55. Howe, M. *Review of the theory of the compression wave generated when a high-speed train enters a tunnel*, Proc Instn Mech Engrs Vol 213 Part F, 1999

56. Vardy, A. & Reinke, P. *Estimation of train resistance coefficients in tunnels from measurements during routine operation*, Proc Instn Mech Engrs Vol 213 Part F, 1999

57. Reinhardt-Piechowiak, A & Ducruet, C. *Inviscid fluid flow around high-speed trains passing by in open air*, Proc Instn Mech Engrs Vol 213 Part F, 1999

58. Tian, HQ. *Formation mechanism of aerodynamic drag of high-speed train and some reduction measures*, Journal of Central South University Technology, (2009) 16: 0166-0171

Index

Lightning Source UK Ltd.
Milton Keynes UK
UKHW020748050721
386649UK00005B/26